This book may be kept
FOURTEEN DAYS

A fine will be charged for each
day the book is kept overtime.

automobile racing

PARAGUAY Gs.18.15
BUGATTI 35B 1929 AEREO

2 DH. POSTAGE
CLAY REGAZZONI /CH
AJMAN

PARAGUAY Gs.0.75
PORSCHE CORREO

10 DH. BLITZEN BENZ
1911
AJMAN POSTAGE

1962 XVᵉ GRAND PRIX AUTOMOBILE
MONACO 1.00

MONACO
0,05 1967
MERCEDES-1936

PARAGUAY Gs.50.00
MERCEDES 1924 AEREO

60 AVUS 1921 1971
DEUTSCHE BUNDESPOST BERLIN

TANZANIA
UGANDA
KENYA Sh.1/30

II JUGOSLOVENSKI ALPSKI RALLYE 1953
70
FNR JUGOSLAVIJA

MONACO
0.01 1967
BUGATTI 1931

XXXIVᵉ RALLYE MONTE CARLO
MINSK
MONTE-CARLO
MONACO 1965 1.00

PARAGUAY Gs.0.20
CARP
BRABHAM CORREO

1 RL AIR MAIL
GRAHAM HILL /GB
AJMAN

PARAGUAY Gs.0.50
MATRA-SIMCA-MS 650 CORREO

PARAGUAY Gs.0.10
FERRARI CORREO

10 DH. اريال ١٠
بريد POSTAGE
JACKIE STEWART GB
AJMAN كجمان

PARAGUAY Gs.0.30
HONDA CORREO

STOCKHOLM 1.00
XXX RALLYE MONTE-CARLO 1961

15 DH. ١٥ درهم
OPEL RACINGCAR
1913/14
AJMAN POSTAGE كجمان

EAST AFRICAN SAFARI RALLY
TANZANIA
UGANDA
KENYA 50

MONACO
0,02 1967
ALFA ROMEO - 1932

PARAGUAY Gs.12.45
MASERATI 8 CTF 1938 AEREO

REPUBLIQUE ISLAMIQUE DE MAURITANIE
POSTE AERIENNE 1969 * COURSE AUTOMOBILE LONDRES-SYDNEY
70F
AUSTRALIE

LESOTHO
12½c ROOF OF AFRICA RALLY 12½c

MANAMA المنامة
DEPENDENCY OF AJMAN
ALFA ROMEO P.2
15 DH. ١٥ درهم
POSTAGE

PARAGUAY Gs.0.15
REPA CORREO

1 DH. ١ درهم
بريد POSTAGE
JACQUES ICKX B
AJMAN كجمان

PARAGUAY Gs.0.25
MARCH CORREO

automobile racing

By Geoffrey Nicholson

PUBLISHERS · GROSSET & DUNLAP · NEW YORK

Contents

Originally titled MOTOR RACING.
Published in the United States by Grosset & Dunlap, Inc.
First printing 1975.

Library of Congress Catalog Card Number 74-17713.
ISBN: 0-448-11784-3 (Trade Edition)
ISBN: 0-448-13250-8 (Library Edition)

Printed in the United States.

How automobile racing began

Automobile racing is almost as old as the car itself. The first car to run on gasoline was built by Carl-Friedrich Benz, who was a German, in 1885. Automobile racing began only ten years later with a race from Paris to Bordeaux and back. A Frenchman, Emile Lavassor, won in a single-cylinder Panhard, which maintained an average speed of 15 miles per hour (or 24 kilometers per hour) over the amazing distance of 732 miles (1,178 kms.).

As each new car was built, the manufacturer would try to prove that it was faster and more reliable than any other by entering it in races. So more and more of these events took place, at first over the dusty and uneven roads which then linked the cities of Europe. Besides hazardous road conditions, there was always danger from straying animals and from spectators accustomed to the slower pace of horse-drawn carriages.

The speeds at which these cars traveled increased with the use of more powerful engines. In fact, they were often too powerful for the light chassis in which they were mounted.

Then disaster struck in the 1903 race from Paris to Madrid. 275 cars and motorcycles started out. By the time the leaders reached Bordeaux — having traveled at an average speed of over 65 m.p.h. (105 k.p.h.) — a series of dreadful accidents had occurred.

At Bordeaux the police decided to stop the race. The cars were towed to the station and sent back to Paris by train.

▲ The finish of the 1901 Paris-Berlin race. The winner was a Frenchman called Fournier who covered the 691 miles (1,112 kms.) at an average speed of 44.4 m.p.h. (71 k.p.h.).

▶ The Gordon Bennett trophy, named after the man who founded the *New York Herald*.

▼ Madame Dugast, the only woman to take part in the 1903 Paris-Madrid race, stopped to nurse drivers who had been injured in crashes.

The move to courses and tracks

The series of accidents which stopped the 1903 Paris-Madrid race changed the future of automobile racing. The sport was banned soon afterwards from the open roads of Europe, and this led to a greater use of road courses and the first special racing tracks.

To organize a race, one had to find quiet country roads which could be closed to other traffic while the event was taking place. This was safer for the drivers and spectators.

Even the biggest events were stopped from using the main roads. In 1902, for instance, the Gordon Bennett Cup race, the most important contest of the time, had been run on the highway from Paris to Innsbruck in Austria. But the next year it had to be held on a ring of little-used roads in Ireland.

In America, too, road courses were used when international races for the Vanderbilt Cup began in 1904. The first race was held on Long Island, near New York, over a bumpy course.

Next came tracks specially built for automobile racing. These began in Great Britain because no racing at all was allowed on public roads.

In 1906 Hugh Locke King built a racing track on his estate in Surrey, near London. It was made of concrete with a distance per lap of 2.67 miles (4.3 kms.) and banking at the turns to allow speeds up to 120 m.p.h. (192 k.p.h.). It was named Brooklands, and remained the home of British motor racing until 1939.

On both sides of the Atlantic

France remained the top car racing nation during the early years of this century, but in America and England, too, the sport was drawing big crowds.

⬆ Louis Wagner, French ace driver

The early Vanderbilt Cup races were held on closed road courses on Long Island where the organizers hoped to avoid accidents by keeping spectators under control. But the popularity of these races grew so quickly that the 1906 event — won by the French ace, Louis Wagner (above) — drew a crowd of over 250,000. Conditions were almost as bad as in the 1903 Paris-Madrid race.

Long Island

Great days at Brooklands

↑← Photographs taken at Brooklands within two years of the opening in 1907 of the world's first track built specially for automobile racing. Women's hats are tied on by scarves to keep them from blowing away in open cars. The visitors at the pit sheds (above) are inspecting a Napier racing car.

Crowds increased after World War 1. (Below left) K. Lee Guinness led the field of 39 cars in the 1924 200-mile (322 kms.) race, was the first driver to win a special badge for lapping the course at 120 m.p.h. (193 k.p.h.).

↓ A handicap race in 1932.

Portrait of a racing driver

Although large crowds turn up for a major race, they see almost nothing of the drivers. The men at the wheel are just a series of heads and shoulders, like wax models hidden beneath helmets. They can be recognized only by their cars or — if you know the sport well — the ways in which they drive.

Inside the cars are men with very different natures, yet at the same time they have much in common.

The typical international racing driver is more intelligent than most people, and knows his own strengths and weaknesses. It would be dangerous if he did not.

Although he drives in a half-lying position, he is by nature an athlete, with quick reactions like a first-class tennis player or football player. Many drivers were very good at other sports before they decided to concentrate on automobile racing.

As a star he is highly paid, but on his way up he earns very little, and he can never be sure of reaching the top. So it must be love of the sport, not money, that spurs him on.

He is well trained. He did not suddenly decide to become a grand prix driver, but worked up to it over the years by driving in other grades of racing.

He likes a challenge, and works best under stress. But though he realizes that racing is dangerous, he is also probably a cautious man. His aim is to keep the danger down to its lowest level by not taking unnecessary risks.

Two masters of motor racing who lived two generations apart

On the face of it, no two racing drivers could be less alike than Rene de Knyff and Jackie Stewart who, 70 years later, has twice been world champion.

Rene de Knyff was a big, bearded Belgian who rarely smiled, while Stewart is a slightly-built Scot who finds it easy to relax.

The Belgian was a pioneer in the days when the sight of an automobile would still make people stand and stare. Stewart grew up in a world where cars were taken for granted.

But read on and you will see that they have much in common . . . particularly their skill as all-around sportsmen, and their determination to succeed.

Rene de Knyff

De Knyff went into the car industry soon after it had started and became the leading driver in France, the country he had chosen to live in. At the same time, he was a director of Panhard-Levassor, the most successful manufacturer in the 1890's. Later he became the chief administrator of auto racing, though he had other keen interests like cycle racing and shooting.

Unlike many of the high-spirited drivers he competed against, de Knyff was known for his sullen expression as he drove to win.

This determination paid off because he won many races, including the 1898 Paris-Bordeaux, the 1899 Spa-Bastogne-Spa and Tour of France, and the 1900 Course of the South-West and the Nice-Marseilles. These were all long road races which were usual at this time.

Jackie Stewart

It is odd that Stewart was also a keen shot before he gave up clay-pigeon shooting for racing. In 1959 and 1960 he was British champion and in the Olympic class.

He, too, worked first on cars — but in the family garage, not in actually building them.

While he is not at all sullen away from the track, he is very serious in his attitude to racing itself.

He won his first Grand Prix at Monza at the end of his opening season as a Formula 1 driver in 1965. Since then he has twice been world champion, in 1969 and 1971, and twice runner-up, in 1968 and 1972.

Safety clothing

In de Knyff's day the racing driver wore a heavy overcoat, often of leather, a scarf, and thick gloves. On his head he had a cap, usually worn backwards, and goggles. His main concern was not with safety but with warmth and comfort. Perched high in the air, with no windshield to protect him, he was exposed to the cold wind, rain and dust.

De Knyff himself had so little fear that he usually set out wearing a soft sailing cap, which would blow off his head before the finish.

Today the driver's body is com-pletely covered in fireproof overalls, and these are usually worn over woollen combinations. His head is protected by a close-fitting fiberglass helmet which comes down to cover his ears and meet his goggles at the front. A mask hides the rest of his face so that none of it is exposed.

Conditions of the track

Stewart drives on a track which has been specially built, or is at least maintained to provide a surface for high speeds. On the latest tracks a high-grip tarmac coating helps road-holding and reduces tire wear.

De Knyff knew nothing like this.

His race tracks were the ordinary earth and gravel roads on which horse-drawn carts had driven for hundreds of years. Because of the ruts left behind by carts and the nails from horses' shoes, there were constant punctures when pneumatic tires were first used in the 1890's.

Great Racing Cars *1. Before World War 1*

These three cars dominated racing in the early years of the century.
The names of the firms that built them are still famous. Each car won the French
Grand Prix when this was regarded as the world championship.

1912 7.6 liter G.P. Peugeot Fitted with twin over-
head camshafts and four valves per cylinder,
which gave it more power for its engine size. In fac
in four years the engine size had almost been

1906 12.9 liter G.P. Renault One of
the earliest racing cars to have a
lightweight pressed-steel chassis,
which was stronger and more rigid
than the older wooden frames.

Driven in the first French Grand Prix at
Le Mans by Ferenc Szisz, it won at an
average speed of 63 m.p.h. (101 k.p.h.)
over 770 miles (1239 kms.),

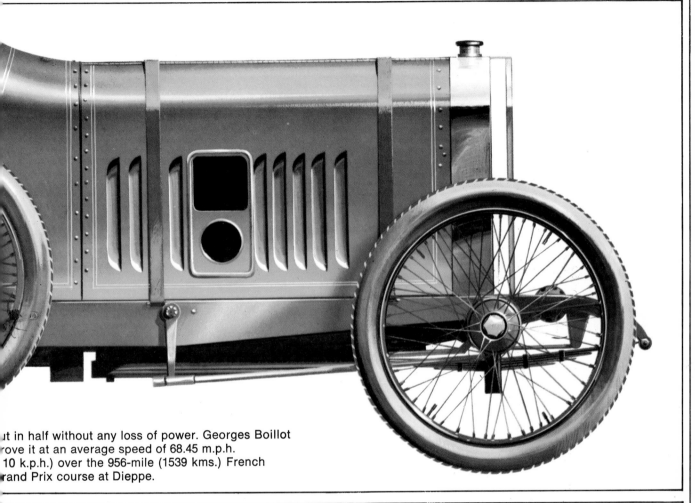

...t in half without any loss of power. Georges Boillot
...rove it at an average speed of 68.45 m.p.h.
...10 k.p.h.) over the 956-mile (1539 kms.) French
...rand Prix course at Dieppe.

1908 12.8 liter G.P. Mercedes This
was an odd but successful mixture of
old-fashioned design — using chain
drive instead of shaft drive — and new
methods. Its four-speed gearbox was
very advanced. Driven by Christian
Lautenschlager, this car won the
477-mile (768 kms.) French Grand Prix
at Dieppe with an average speed of
69 m.p.h. (111 k.p.h.).

Automobile racing today

In the early days you might have found cars with steam, electric and gasoline engines in the same race. This would not be possible today. There are now many different types of racing, and each has its own set of rules.

Probably the most important of these rules lays down the maximum size of engine which the car may have. There are other rules about the kind of engine which is allowed, the overall weight of the car, the amount of fuel to be carried, the length of the wheelbase, and so on, down to minor mechanical details. In other areas the designers have a free choice. The set of rules for a particular type of racing is known as the formula.

The reason for having a formula is to set designers the same basic problem to solve. Within the limits laid down by the rules, they must use their skill to find ways of making their car faster and more reliable than their rivals' cars.

Having a formula also helps the drivers. Since their cars are alike — though never exactly the same — they can only win races by being better drivers than their rivals.

The first formula was used for the French Grand Prix of 1906, and the French continued to draw up the rules for grand prix racing until 1922. The job was then taken over by the world governing body, now called the *Federation Internationale de l'Automobile;* it is usually known by its initials, FIA. Today there are both international and national formulas with rules for almost every class of racing.

Formula for an open race

The formulas for the different types and classes of racing are enough to fill a very large book. Here is a guide to fourteen of the most important of them.

Formula 1 The 3-liter formula for grand prix racing. Engines must have power units of 3000 c.c. unsupercharged or 1500 c.c. supercharged (see Glossary, page 59); cylinders limited to twelve. New rules for 1973 raised minimum weight to 575 kg. (1267.7 lbs.) and made stronger safety measures. World championship Formula 1 race must be between 250 kms. (155.3 miles) and 525 kms. (201.9 miles) in length.

Formula Atlantic A British-based formula midway between Formulas 3 and 2. It was brought in at the start of the 1971 season for club events, but was used for the first time in international races during 1973. In the United States a similar Formula B is run.

Formula Ford The most popular of all formulas for cheaper single-seat racing, it is based on the use of the 1600 c.c. Ford Cortina GT engine, slightly modified. Spread from Britain all over the world.

Group 5 Sports Cars These are the cars which compete in such long-distance races as the Le Mans 24-hours and Nürburgring 1000 kms. (621.4 miles). In world championship events they are limited to engines with a capcity of 3000 c.c.

Grand Touring Cars While prototypes can compete in Group 5, the machines in GT racing must be production cars. Group 3 is open to Production GT cars of which at least one thousand must have been built; they can be only slightly modified. Group 4 are modified "specials," but at least 500 must be built.

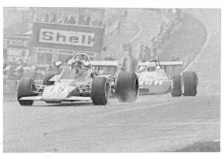

Formula 2 Produces the "second division" racing for drivers who hope to get into the grand prix class. The 1972 formula, due to run until the end of the 1975 season, is for 2000 c.c. engines; no supercharging. From January, 1974, weight limit for all cars to be 475 kg. (1047 lbs.). Maximum length for any Formula 2 race is 250 km. (155.3 miles).

Formula 3 The formula for lower-cost international racing. It is for cars with four-cylinder engines, but limit of 1600 c.c. will be raised to 2000 c.c. at the end of 1975. No supercharging is allowed. Minimum weight is 440 kgs. (970 lbs.).

Formula 5000 This formula was brought in — at first in the United States as Formula A — to encourage single-seat racing in the grand prix style, but using cheaper 5000 c.c. V8 production engines. The engines can be modified, and the best of them will produce over 500 b.h.p., which is roughly 20 b.h.p. more than the top Formula 1 cars.

Formula Vee/Super Vee Like Formula Ford, this is based on a single company's engines — Vee uses the 1200 c.c. and 1300 c.c. Volkswagen Beetle sedan engines, and Super Vee the 1600 c.c. VW engine. The formula began in the United States with help from the German manufacturers. To keep costs down, it insists that VW transmission and brakes be used.

U.S.A.C. National Championship Formula The most powerful single-seater racing machines in the world. Several types of engines are allowed; the Offenhauser develops more than 800 b.h.p. Racing is on oval tracks and cars may reach over 200 m.p.h. (321.9 k.p.h.).

Group 7 Sports Cars This group is used in the Can-Am series, and covers cars which have two-seater bodies but otherwise are pure racing machines. There is no limit on engine capacity, and some cars are able to develop 900 b.h.p. or more.

Sedan Cars In Britain these compete in two groups. Special sedan cars are allowed a number of modifications, and even a different engine, as long as the outline remains the same. Standard production sedans are very little altered except for safety measures.

Stock Cars — United States Here the term "stock" means standard, and covers racing between production cars which were not built for competition. They are allowed a number of modifications, however, and are made stronger in case of accidents on the short oval tracks.

Stock Cars — European In Britain and parts of Europe a stock car is a single-seater sedan which only looks like a production model. During a race the cars try to bump each other off the track. In Scandinavia stock car races often take place on frozen lakes.

Profile of a racing course

Grand prix events and the big long-distance races like the Le Mans 24-hour and the Indianapolis 500 attract large crowds. Often 80,000 people turn up at the Monza track in Italy, 100,000 at Silverstone in the Midlands of England, and 350,000 at the Nürburgring or Indianapolis. Everything is organized perfectly to keep the spectators safe and satisfied.

A grand prix race, which is run over 190-310 miles (300-500 km.), will last only a few hours. But two days are set aside beforehand for practice, and afterwards there is a lot of clearing up to be done, so that the course is in fact being used heavily for over a week. A thousand people or so are involved behind the scenes of every grand prix, including the office staff, gatemen, program sellers and marshals.

Then there is the medical staff. 30 or more doctors stand by, helped by a team of nurses and students. One doctor remains at each corner throughout the race, while others attend first-aid units and the mobile hospital housed in a giant trailer.

During the race there will be at least one big fire engine and several smaller ones at the ready, supported by breakdown trucks, in case there is a serious accident.

For the actual running of the race, the clerk of the course has about seven scrutineers to check the cars, nine timekeepers, and various marshals, each with special duties, at the corners and in the pits.

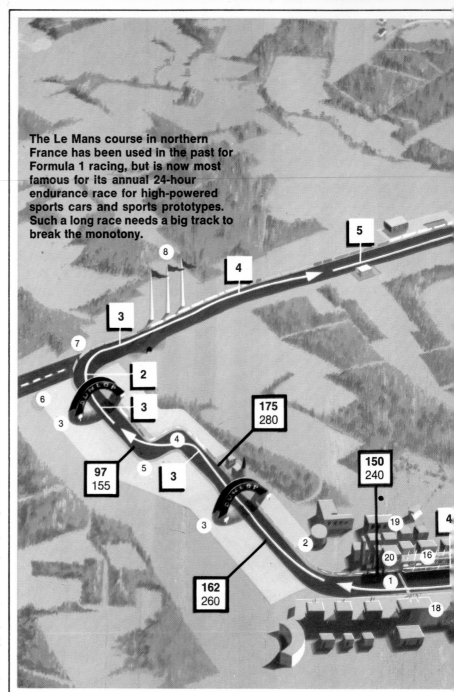

The Le Mans course in northern France has been used in the past for Formula 1 racing, but is now most famous for its annual 24-hour endurance race for high-powered sports cars and sports prototypes. Such a long race needs a big track to break the monotony.

1 Starting line and grid
2 Popular enclosure
3 Dunlop footbridges which allow spectators to reach the center
4 The Esses
5 Amusement area, brightly lit up during the night of the 24-hour race
6 Road to the town of Le Mans
7 Tertre Rouge (Red Hill) corner
8 Wind-direction flags which tell the drivers whether it is best to take the right or left side of the straight
9 Hunaudieres Straight: the fastest stretch of the circuit, where speeds of up to 230 m.p.h. (370 k.p.h.) are recorded
10 Road to Tours; Mulsanne bend
11 Arnage bend
12 Indianapolis bend
13 Maison Blanche (White House)
14 Finishing line. When the winner crosses this at the end of the 24-hour race he will have covered over 1000 miles (1610 kms.)
15 The pits
16 Pit balcony boxes for sponsors and officials; race offices
17 Scene of the world's worst racing disaster, in 1955, when one driver and 80 spectators were killed
18 Main grandstand
19 The Village — a group of cafes, shops and trade exhibition stands
20 Control box

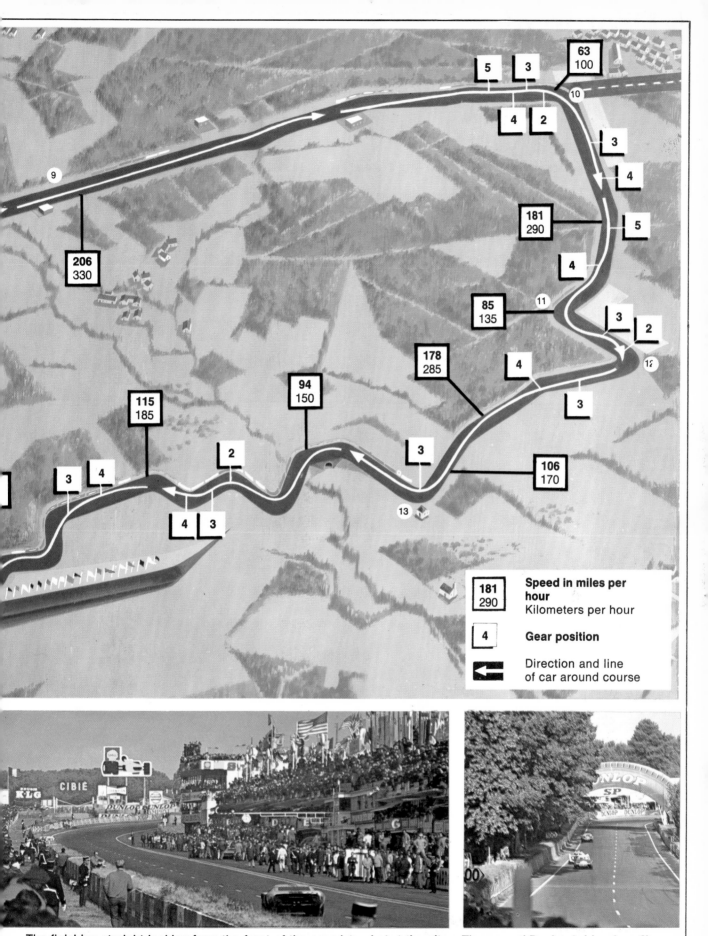

| 63 | 5 | 3 |
| 100 | | |

| 4 | 2 |

| 3 |

9

| 4 |

| 206 | 181 | 5 |
| 330 | 290 | |

| 4 |

| 85 | 11 | 3 | 2 |
| 135 | | | |

| 178 |
| 285 |

| 4 |

| 94 | 3 |
| 150 | |

| 115 | 2 | 3 |
| 185 | | |

| 106 |
| 170 |

| 3 | 4 |

| 4 | 3 |

13

181
290

Speed in miles per hour
Kilometers per hour

4

Gear position

◄ Direction and line of car around course

The finishing straight looking from the front of the grandstand past the pits

The second Dunlop bridge (see 3)

17

Major tracks of the world

The racing tracks built before World War I — like Brooklands in England and Indianapolis in the United States — were roughly oval or egg-shaped. They were specially designed for the drivers to show how fast their cars could travel. The longer, straighter sections of the track were flat, but the turns were built at a slope so that the cars could be driven around this banking at high speeds. This type of track is often called a speedway.

In the 1920's a different kind of track became popular in Europe. It was more like an ordinary public road with turns and corners, hills and dips, broad and narrow sections. The cars had to go slower here than on an oval course, but it was a better test of their steering, braking and suspension systems, and of the drivers' skill and concentration.

A good example is the Nürburgring in the Eifel mountains of Germany. It was built between 1925 and 1927.

The course was shaped like a figure-8 to give one large circuit of 14.19 miles (22.8 km.) and a smaller one of 4.8 miles (7.7 km.). As it followed the natural shape of the hills and valleys, it had 174 turns. But at one famous hairpin turn, called the Karussell, it also had special banking, like a speedway track.

Since the 1920's many tracks have been built — most of them road courses, although speedways remain popular in the United States. No two tracks are alike, and the difference between them adds to the interest of racing.

Brickyard to harbor wall

Every racing course ever built, from Aintree to Zolder, has something interesting about it. Here we describe what makes five of the world's most famous tracks different from all the others.

Monaco
Some major races are still run on public roads. The most famous one of all is the Monaco Grand Prix, which began in 1929. Its 1.95-mile (3.145 kms.) course runs through the city streets of Monaco.

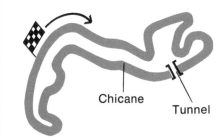
Chicane — Tunnel

Silverstone
During World War 2 an airplane manufacturing plant was built over the famous British racing course at Brooklands. So after the war the Royal Automobile Club had to find somewhere else to race. It looked at a number of airfields which had been used by the RAF and had now gone out of use. There were many reasons why these would have made good courses. They were big; they had runways which could be used as the basis for racing tracks; and they were usually built many miles away from big towns, so that the noise of racing would not upset anyone. The airfield chosen by the RAC was near the Northamptonshire village of Silverstone. It now has a course of three miles (4.83 kms.).

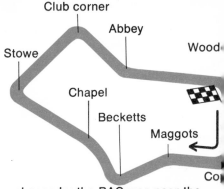
Club corner — Abbey — Wood — Stowe — Chapel — Becketts — Maggots — Co

Indianapolis

Why is Indianapolis, the oldest racing course still in use, known all over the world as the Brickyard? The explanation goes back to 1909 when the 2$\frac{1}{2}$ mile (4.023 kms.) course was laid out in the shape of a rectangle with curved corners. At once the surface of gravel, tar and limestone began to crumble from the wear of the tires; so in the same year 3,200,000 paving bricks were laid on top of it. The track has since been given a new surface so that only the starting line is now marked by a line of bricks, but to

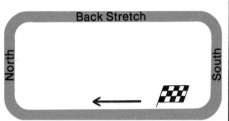

all racing fans it is still known as the Brickyard. Its most famous event is the 500-mile race, which was first run in 1911 and which has taken place every year since then except during the two World Wars.

aul Ricard Course

uilt in 1970 by the French millionaire fter whom it is named, the Paul icard course is the most modern and e safest in the world. After M. Ricard ad bought the site — an area of ocky barren land in the hot, dry hills ear Toulon — he asked leading rench drivers to help him design the est course possible. Everything has een done to make the track safe. here are escape routes which the river can take if he fails to get around e sharp corners, as well as miles f wire-netting and safety barriers eside the track. The total length of e course, which will be used for

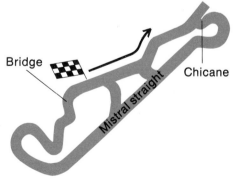

grand prix races, is 3.6 miles (5.8 kms.), but it can be split up into two smaller courses for less important events and for learners.

Zandvoort

The racing course at Zandvoort, a seaside town on the Dutch coast, was laid out on roads built by the Germans during World War 2.

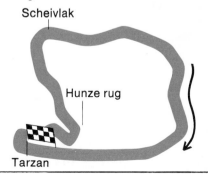

The driver depends on his team

A driver may have skill and courage, but he will not win any races unless his car is running perfectly. So a great deal depends on the team of mechanics who look after it. Before the start they do all the last-minute jobs, like tuning the engine, in a place near the starting line called the paddock. During the race itself they work in special places at the side of the track called the "pits."

For the 1908 French Grand Prix real pits were dug into the ground so that the mechanics could get underneath the cars, and though this is no longer done, the name has stuck. It is in these pits that vital work is carried out during the race. They are protected by a crash barrier from any cars that might spin off the track.

From here signals are given to the driver telling him his position in the race, and the mechanics wait at the ready to refuel the car and carry out repairs. In a short race of less than 300 miles, the driver will stop here only if something has gone wrong, but in a longer one he will need to fill up at some stage. With a good team of mechanics, who have been trained against the stopwatch, this need take only half a minute.

In a really long race he will need to make regular stops, not only for gasoline and oil, but also for new tires and brake pads. It is here that the skill of the mechanics comes in, because they can help to save vital seconds for their driver. A well-trained team might take only 1½ or 2 minutes on these jobs.

Not a second to lose

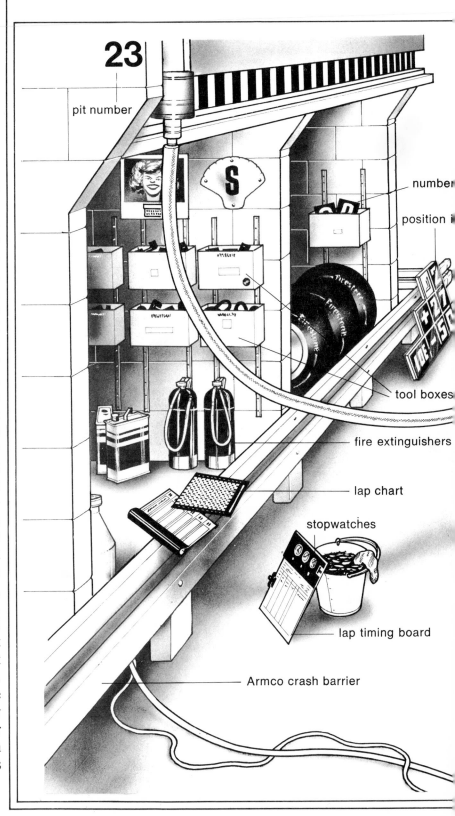

23

pit number

number

position i

tool boxes

fire extinguishers

lap chart

stopwatches

lap timing board

Armco crash barrier

A team manager's plan, drawn up for the 1955 Tourist Trophy, shows how the pit routine is worked out so that no second is lost. The driver stops right on the white line, and the mechanics move steadily from one job to the next. They could change four wheels, take on 30 gallons (136 liters) of fuel, and add oil and water in 70 seconds.

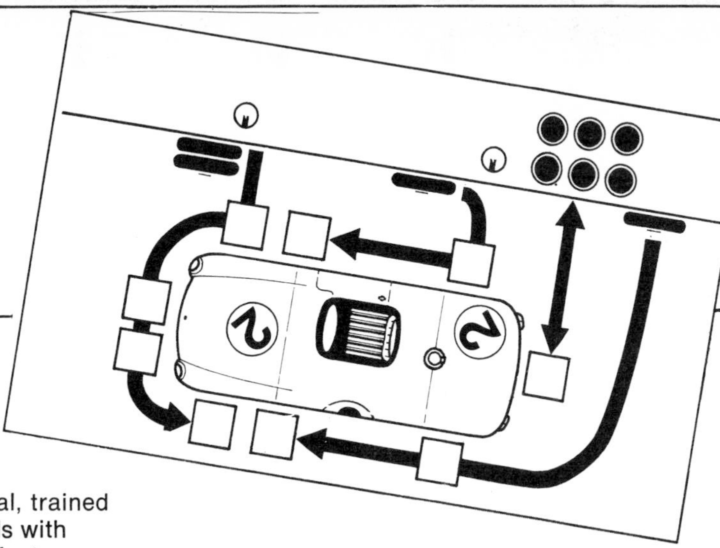

Pit stop for a 312P Ferrari during the world sports-car championships, and the mechanics go through a carefully worked-out routine of refueling and changing tires.

seconds ahead of the fifth man

seconds behind the third man

volunteer fire marshal, trained by fire service, stands with extinguishers at his feet

aluminized asbestos suit

driver strapped in by team-mate — straps too tight for him to do up himself

aluminum fuel churn, specially vented for quick filling

mechanic, usually in his twenties, but with at least five years' apprenticeship behind him.

pneumatic wrench to undo bolts

footwear prevent sparks

pressure hose for quick filling — about 30 gallons (135 liters) per minute

quick-lift jack

wide racing tire with pressure about 14 lbs. per sq. in.

Great Racing Cars *2. Between the wars*

Between the wars there was a period known as the Depression. It lasted from the late 1920's to the middle of the 1930's. Many manufacturers did not have the money to back grand prix racing. Even so, it was at this time that these three famous cars were built.

1930 Bentley 4¹/₂ liter supercharged. The 4¹/₂ liter sports car, designed by W. O. Bentley, was built for the Le Mans 24-hour race, which it won in 1928. The supercharged version of the car, which was developed by Sir Henry Birkin, was even more powerful. Competing against grand prix racing cars in the French G.P. at Pau in 1930, Sir Henry claimed to have reached 135 m.p.h. (217.26 k.p.h.) and took second place in the event.

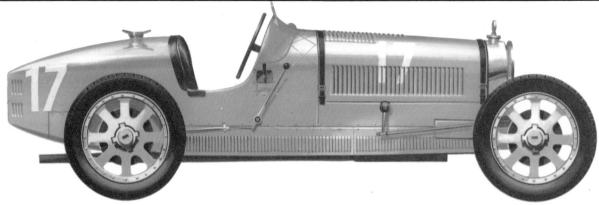

Bugatti T35   The most successful grand prix car of the period, it had many brilliant details in its design (by Ettore Bugatti) as well as a high standard of engineering work. It first appeared in 1925 and dominated grand prix racing for most of the next six years. The car was widely sold to amateur drivers, and it is said to have won over 1,000 victories.

Mercedes-Benz W125 Was the most powerful grand prix car ever built. It raced only during the 1937 season, winning seven grand prix compared with the five wins of its close German rivals, Auto-Union. Its chassis and suspension design were based on new ideas, and influenced the minds of racing car designers for the next 20 years.

How to watch a race

You may find your first visit to a automobile race confusing. The cars pass by so quickly that it is not always easy to spot the leader. You will probably wonder why the officials are waving different colored flags, and why the crowd is suddenly so excited. But the more you learn about the sport, the more interesting it will become.

You will get to recognize the cars and their drivers, and be able to tell those that are leading from those a lap or more behind. And you will know that if the marshal is waving a red and yellow flag, for instance, he is telling the drivers that the road ahead is very slippery.

In time, too, you will begin to admire the special skills of the different drivers as they control the drift of their cars around a turn or pick the right moment to overtake the car in front.

First of all, however, you should make sure that you can follow the progress of the race you have come to see. And for that you must do some homework — but of a very enjoyable kind. For one thing, you must get to know the cars and the drivers. The best place to do this is at the paddock, where the mechanics work on the cars before the race. There you can learn to spot the cars of each team by their colors and markings. You will also be able to see what the drivers look like without their helmets.

Then, when the race begins, you can keep your own record of it with a lap chart. We show you how to make one, and fill it in, on the right.

Points to watch

From the national flag which starts a race to the checkered flag which ends it, there is always something to look out for. The drivers have the busiest time, of course. But if you look at the way they corner, watch for the marshals' signals, and keep your lap chart up to date, you won't have a spare moment either.

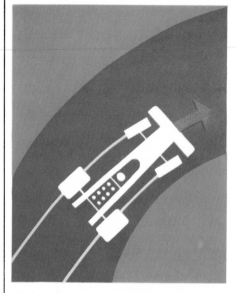 

Sliding through corners
When a car is driven slowly around a bend, it stays almost parallel with the inside of the curve. But when it is driven at speed in a race, the front wheels are turned in as if the car was being pointed at the inside of the

curve. And the back wheels slide away from it. In fact, the car is made to drift slightly sideways on all four wheels as it takes the corner. Keeping this drift under control is one of the great skills of racing.

➡ Make your own lap chart
To follow the way in which a race is going, keep a lap chart. At big races you may find a chart in the program, but for smaller races you will need to make your own. You will need as many squares across as there are laps in the race, and as many squares down as there are cars.

At the end of lap 1, fill in the car numbers, in the order in which they crossed the line, down the first column on the left. Fill in the next column at the end of lap 2, and so on. In our chart taken from the 1972 Spanish Grand Prix, you can see that Hulme led for the first four laps, Stewart for the next four, and Fittipaldi took over on lap 9.

LAP CHART

RACE	LAP RECORD	RACE DISTANCE
SPANISH GP	1 MIN 24·30 Sec	190·15 MILES

DATE	LAP DISTANCE	START TIME
MAY 1 1972	2·115 MILES	15.00 HRS

CIRCUIT	LAPS	WEATHER
JARAMA	90	FINE, HOT

No.	DRIVER/CAR	LAPS													
		1	2	3	4	5	6	7	8	9	10	11	12	13	14
11	D. HULME	11	11	11	11	1	1	1	1	5	5	5	5	5	5
1	J. STEWART	1	1	1	1	11	5	5	5	1	1	1	1	1	1
6	C. REGAZZONI	6	4	4	4	4	4	4	4	4	4	4	4	4	4
4	J. ICKX	4	6	5	5	5	11	11	11	11	11	11	11	11	11
5	E. FITTIPALDI	5	5	6	6	6	6	6	6	6	7	7	7	7	7
7	M. AND	7	19	19	7	7	7	7	7	6	6	6	6	6	
												9	9	9	9

Slipstreaming

During the race a slower car can often keep pace with one that is faster simply by driving just behind it. The front car then shelters the second car by breaking the air resistance, and so gives it a tow. Driving behind another car to get this kind of help is known as "slipstreaming."

National flag
The national flag of the country in which the race is taking place is used to signal the start.

White flag
Warning that ambulance or rescue truck is on the course. If waved, it means that this vehicle is just ahead.

Blue flag
When held still by a marshal, it tells the driver that another car is close behind him. When it is waved, it means that the car behind is closing up fast or trying to overtake.

Black flag
Held up with a board showing the car number. The Clerk of the Course is ordering the driver to stop at the pits next time — to be warned about driving wrongly or because his car may be in a dangerous condition.

Yellow flag
Held still by marshal, it means that there is some danger ahead, perhaps something in the way. Waved, it means that there is greater danger. Driver must slow down and be ready to stop.

Red flag
All cars must stop at once.

Yellow and red flag
Warning of slippery surface ahead, probably from oil on the track. If waved, means that the track is very slippery.

Checkered flag
Waved for the winner as he crosses the finish line. Held still for following cars to show that the race is over.

Take your camera along

Going to a race is much more fun if you make your own record of the event. You can do this either with a camera or a sketchpad (you will find more about sketching and painting on another page).

You don't need an expensive camera to take good photographs of the racing scene. In fact, you can even get exciting *action* pictures with a slow-speed camera — as long as you take a couple of tips from professional photographers.

First, choose a spot on the course where the cars are not going at top speed. Then pick out one car and, as it drives past, swing your camera with it, keeping the car in the middle of the viewfinder. This action is known as "panning."

Try panning a few times until you find that you can do it without losing the car. Next time click the shutter. You should have a picture in which the car itself is sharp and clear, but the background is blurred. This makes the photograph look even more lifelike because it shows that the car is traveling really fast.

Another time, find a place on a corner where the cars are coming toward you. Head-on movement is much easier to "stop" with an ordinary camera.

Don't just look for action pictures, though, There are many other things worth noticing at the paddock and the pits. Try building up a complete record of all the color and variety that makes up a day at the course.

Keep your finger on the button

These interesting photographs, taken by professionals, have two lessons to teach the amateur. The first is: Always look for the unexpected picture. The second: Be Prepared.

You never know when some unexpected incident will happen. Because he was on the alert, the photographer caught this wheel coming off.

35mm. cassette
The type of film used by most serious photographers.

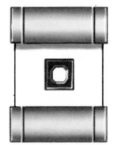

Film cartridge
Now used more often than the roll film, it can be instantly loaded into the camera, and you don't have to wind the film back after use.

Roll film
This was once the most popular type of film. It has a paper backing so that light cannot damage it by accident.

1 Knob for winding the film.
2 Button you press to take photogr
3 Viewfinder which shows you your picture.
4 The controls for focusing and for choosing the lens aperture

n't merely photograph the racing.
ok for unusual pictures of the crowds.

Often an accident is worth a series of pictures. Speed with shutter and the film-transport lever resulted in this picture story of a crash.

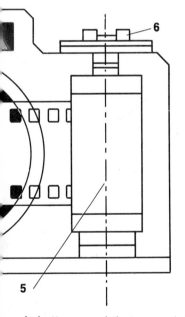

and shutter speed that control the amount of light let in, are often on the side of lens.
Metal cassette which holds the film.
Knob for winding film back into cassette.

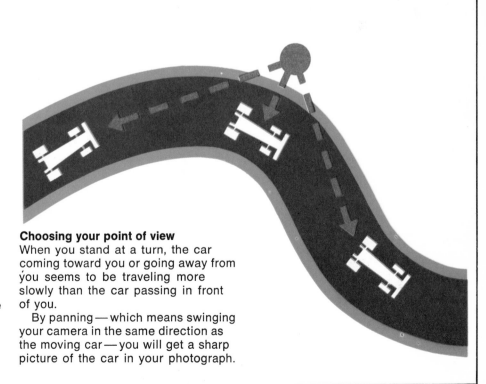

Choosing your point of view
When you stand at a turn, the car coming toward you or going away from you seems to be traveling more slowly than the car passing in front of you.

By panning — which means swinging your camera in the same direction as the moving car — you will get a sharp picture of the car in your photograph.

Sketch at haste, paint at leisure

There is a special secret in getting good drawings and paintings of racing. You must get into the habit of using your sketching pad as a notebook, and practice making your notes quickly and accurately.

You will soon see the reason for this. When you are painting the view from your bedroom window, for instance, you can take as long as you like over it, and return to it any time you wish. And probably nobody will disturb you while you are working at your picture. But an automobile race lasts only a few hours, so you must work fast. And you will have the crowds moving around you all the while.

So instead of trying to complete your picture at the course, use these few crowded hours for making notes. Sketch in your pad the angle of a car as it takes a corner, the position of the driver in his cockpit, the details of a particular part of the car, the way a mechanic bends down to change a wheel. If your notebook is filled with these jottings, you will be able to put a more careful picture together when you get home.

The simplest and most useful tool for sketching is, of course, a pencil. But you can use pen and ink to make your drawings stronger, and felt pens to remind you of the colors.

You can take the chance of working in water colors or oils, but you'll have to choose the time and place carefully.

Take a pad and a pencil

All you need for a day's sketching: spiral-bound pad; 2B pencil with sharpener or knife and soft eraser; felt tip pens for coloring; pen and waterproof ink to draw outlines; carpenter's pencil for shading.

How and what to note
You will probably not have time to make a complete picture, so use your sketch pad to collect the details you will need later on. When you come to paint your racing scene, it is the details which will bring the picture to life.

How to draw a racing car

Formula 1
1 First draw a horizontal line. At either end put the wheels. See that they are the right size and distance apart.

Sports Car
1 Start as before by drawing the wheels on a horizontal line. Add your rectangle to show height and length.

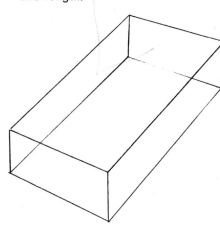

Three-dimensional drawing
1 Measure the length, height and width of the car, and draw a rectangular box in the same proportions.

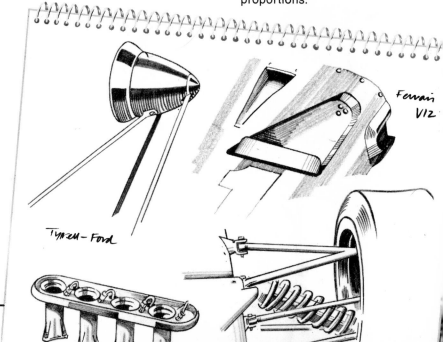

Ferrari V12

Tyrrell-Ford

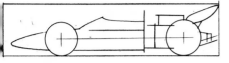

2 Draw a rectangle around them to give yourself a guide to the height and length of the car. Sketch the outline.

3 Put in the position of the driver's cockpit and the engine, and make your rough outline more exact.

4 Add the driver and fill in the other details, including the race number. Finally, erase your guide lines.

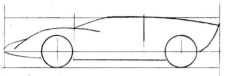
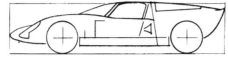

2 After you have sketched the rough outline of the car, draw two vertical lines to show the length of the cab.

3 Between these two lines put in the shapes of the windows. Add any of the major details.

4 Once more the last stage is to add the finer detail, make the outline stronger and remove the guide lines.

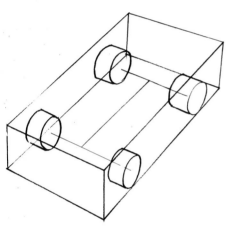
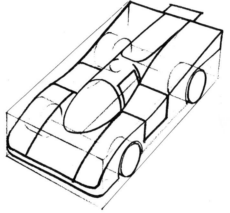
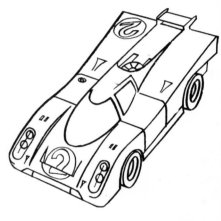

2 Sketch in all four wheels. This will help you to "see" the car more clearly and get things in the right place.

3 Draw in the outline of the nearer side, then of the far side. Windows give you the lines across the car.

4 Once the overall shape is correct, you will be able to add the detail. Finally, strengthen and clean up the drawing.

The finishing touch
Having learned to draw a racing car by this method, you can then use the note from your sketch pad to complete the picture.

The cost of grand prix racing

The dozen teams that compete in the Formula I world championship spend over seven million dollars between them each year. That means that each team will pay out about $625,000 just to race two cars. It seems a huge figure until you consider the number of men who support the driver and the cost of putting cars that are in perfect racing order on the track.

A typical support team is made up of eleven people. There are six mechanics — two each for the two cars that will compete and two more for the car kept in reserve. One man looks after the spares, and another, called a fabricator, makes the spare parts which are not standard and cannot be bought. Then there are the manager, his assistant and a secretary.

Their wages add up to about $50,000, and the fees of the main driver will be at least double that figure. In fact, in a year one of the stars of grand prix racing may be paid over $250,000 to drive. Strangely enough, the second driver will probably not be paid at all. He may even have to pay as much as $100,000 for his place in the team. This money comes from personal sponsors, probably in the automobile industry.

Most of the team must fly to 14 to 15 countries during the season, while the cars and their transporter must sometimes be sent by ship. That puts another $65,000 or $75,000 on the bill. Then there are the costs of running a workshop and office even before you start to count the expense of building and running the cars themselves.

Where the money goes

In the early 1960s it was possible to buy a ready-built Formula 1 car for about $18,000 and have some success with it. In fact, in 1959 Cooper won their first world championship with a

car that cost under $10,000 to build, fitted with a $3,000 engine. Today success costs ten times as much.

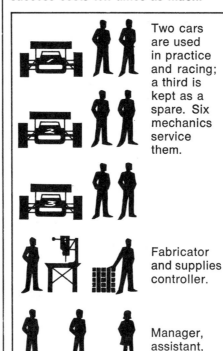

Two cars are used in practice and racing; a third is kept as a spare. Six mechanics service them.

Fabricator and supplies controller.

Manager, assistant, secretary.

⬆ Support team
This is the team behind the team. And, of course, these eleven people do not include the ones who stay at home and look after the works.

⬇ The driver and his car
The team's leading driver will probably be paid between $125,000 and $250,000 a year because he has proved that he can win grand prix races. The first car that is ready to race costs about $62,500 to build. This includes design work in the drawing office, making special machine tools, testing and development. Later copies of this model cost only $18,500. But all these figures do not include the engine and gearbox.

⬧ Transporter and van
A racing car cannot be driven to the course, so the team's two competing cars and the spare must travel by transporter. This will cost about $20,000 to buy. The team must also take its own tools and spares to the course. The van and the driver to carry out this job add another $5,000 to the running costs.

⬧ ⬆ Engine and gearbox
If bought, an engine comes to about $18,500, but if specially made, it is more expensive. A team with three cars will buy six engines at the start of a season. Each car uses two engines at an event — one for practice, the other for the race. The gearbox costs an additional $1,325 or so.

⬆ Wheels and tires
The magnesium wheels cost $300 each; a single car will use eight to twelve of these during a race. Tires are only $90 each — but 200 of them may be used in a season, so the bill soon adds up to $18,000. These tires get a lot of hard wear; and also, those used on fast courses will not be suitable for slow ones.

⬧ Engine servicing
An ordinary motorist has his car serviced every 5,000 or 6,000 miles. But a racing team sends its engines back to the manufacturer for checking over and rebuilding after each race. So every engine is serviced fifteen times a season. This costs the team over $45,000 a year.

Where the money comes from

Part of every team's running costs is met by the people who organize the grand prix races. In Europe each organizer contributes $110,000 to divide among the teams, according to how they get on in the race. Out of this sum come the prizes — starting at about $6,200 for first place, and going down to as little as $250 for the twentieth car to cross the line. U.S. and South African organizers must offer higher prizes in order to attract teams from Europe.

Yet even the most successful team could not pay its way out of its winnings and bonuses alone. To survive, it must have the backing of various companies who give the team money in the hope of getting useful publicity for their products in return.

Most of them are connected in some way with the automobile industry. In return for sponsorship, the cars in the team carry labels, known as decals, displaying the company's name or a product. Tire companies are the most important; their contract may be worth $65,000 to the team. Then come the gasoline companies and makers of parts like spark plugs and brake linings; these together may add another $38,000.

Recently, however, the biggest sponsors have come from outside the automobile industry. Cigarette manufacturers, for instance, are now banned from advertising their products on television because smoking is dangerous to health. So instead they link their names with a fast, exciting sport, and will pay up to $250,000 a year to do this.

Sponsors say look for the label

In most cases the reward for sponsorship is a label on the body of the car — or upon clothes worn by drivers and mechanics. However, some of the big sponsors from outside the automobile industry like to have their name included in the name of the car itself. So you get race entries like John Player Special, the Brooke Bond Oxo-Rob Walker-Surtees and the Yardley-McLaren. Shown here are some of the sponsors who now keep grand prix racing going.

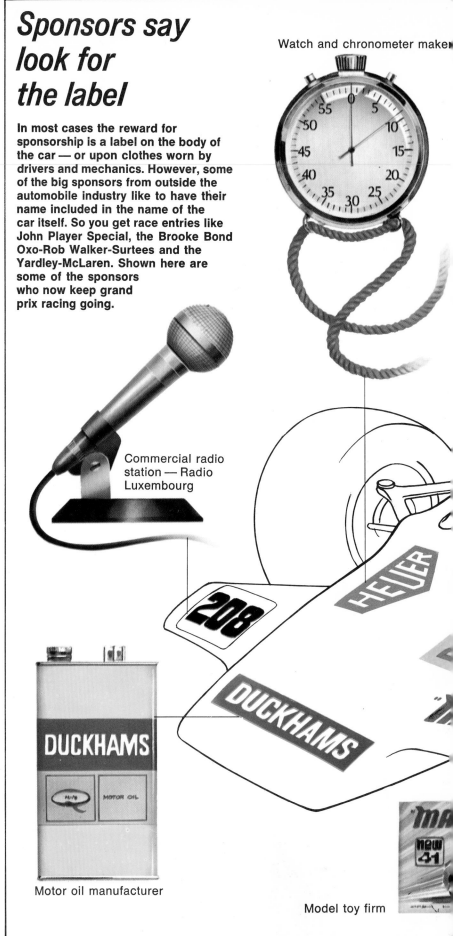

Watch and chronometer maker

Commercial radio station — Radio Luxembourg

Motor oil manufacturer

Model toy firm

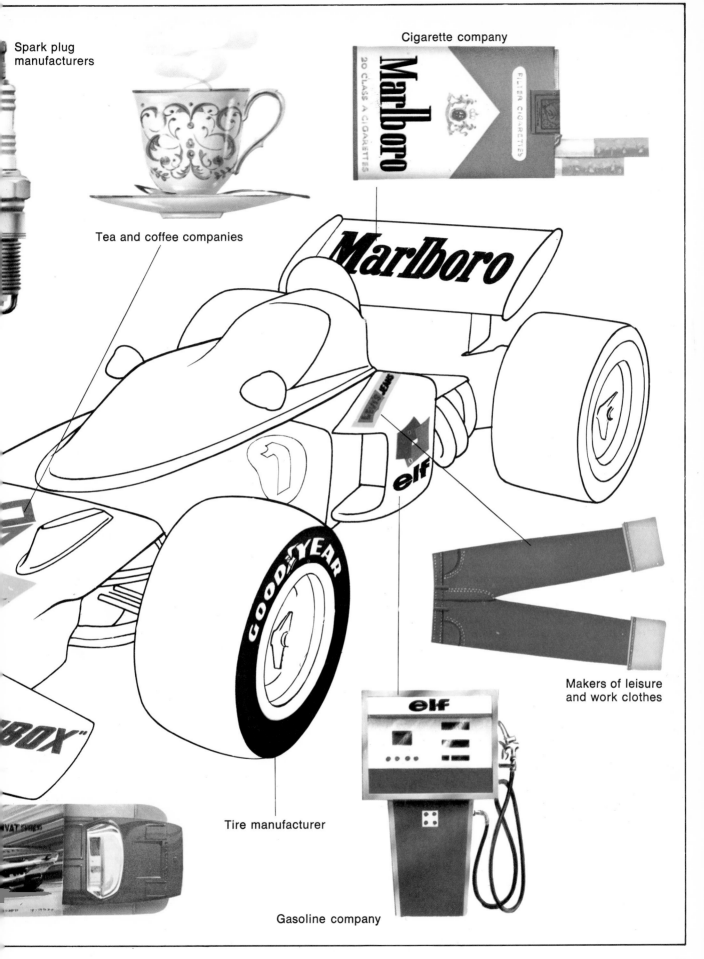

Spark plug manufacturers

Tea and coffee companies

Cigarette company

Makers of leisure and work clothes

Tire manufacturer

Gasoline company

Great Racing Cars   *3. After World War 2*

Italy was the first auto-racing nation to recover from the effects of World War II, and shortly after it her cars won almost all the grand prix events. By the early 1950's, however, the British Jaguar was having considerable success in the Le Mans 24-hour race.

Alfa Romeo 158 This was the most successful grand prix car of the period just after the war — partly because it had already proved its value earlier. At that time it had been built for "voiturette" racing — what we now call Formula 2. In 1946 it took part in grand prix races, and was the most efficient machine for the next six years.

Maserati 250F This car was driven by the great Fangio. It won its first race, the 1954 Argentine Grand Prix, and went on to take many of the bigger prizes over the next four years. 1957 was the car's finest year, giving Fangio the world championship for drivers.

Jaguar D Type   The Jaguar C Type had already won the Le Mans 24-hour in 1951 and 1953, but the improved D Type turned out to be even more successful. It won three victories in a row in the years 1955-7. Its greatest triumph was in 1957 when five D-Types finished first, second, third, fourth and sixth.

Grand prix racing — a world apart

A Formula I racing car is in a different class from the ordinary car. Its design and manufacture have as little to do with the mass production of everyday cars as a racehorse has to do with a horse that works on a farm.

This was not always so. The early manufacturers entered races to advertise the models which they hoped to sell in their showrooms. And even after cars appeared which had been specially built for racing, they still had a strong link with ordinary models. New ideas were tried out during races and, if they worked, passed on to the family car.

Yet look again at the three cars illustrated on pages 12 and 13. You will probably find their names familiar. These firms still build cars, but they have almost completely given up their connection with grand prix racing.

Peugeot was the first to drop out, and Mercedes the last, as recently as 1955. Only Renault is still involved in racing, but even this is through their Alpine company, not in their own name. In fact, the three companies now concentrate on making cars for the general public, though they still enter rallies.

New names, such as March, Brabham and McLaren, have taken their place in the sport, and these have little connection with the ordinary automobile industry. They manufacture cars strictly for racing. The two worlds have moved apart.

Look at the McLaren on the right. You will see that it differs not only in shape from the family car, it differs in almost every detail.

X-ray view of the modern racing car

The Yardley-McLaren is here stripped down to show you what lies beneath the streamlined body of today's Formula 1 racing car. You can see how each of the main parts serves a particular purpose. With this car the McLaren team had the best reliability record of 1972. From 25 grand prix starts, their cars finished in the first six 16 times, including a win in the South African Grand Prix for Denny Hulme.

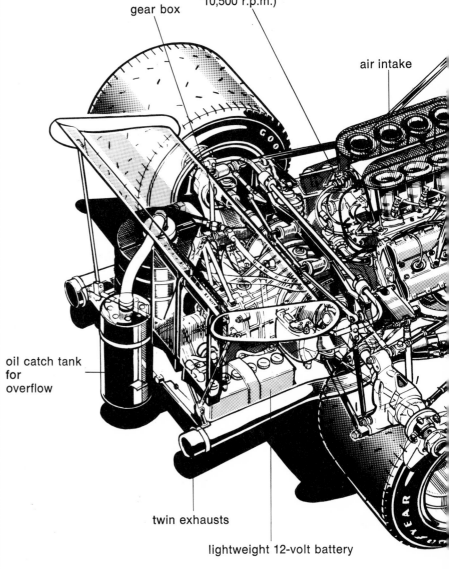

monocoque chassis made from gl and rivetted sheet alloy. The front rear airplane-type sections of the c are bolted to this

Cosworth-Ford V-8 DFV (double four valve) 3 liter engine (440 h.p., 10,500 r.p.m.)

gear box

air intake

oil catch tank for overflow

twin exhausts

lightweight 12-volt battery

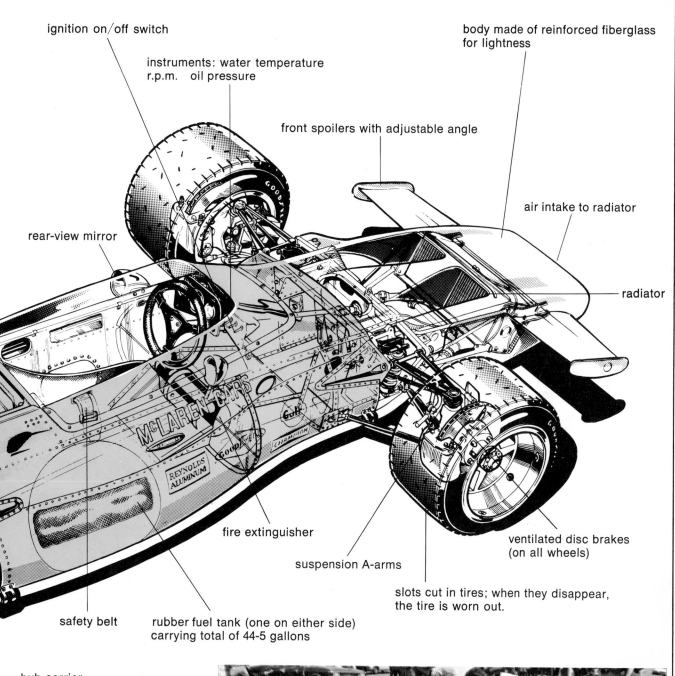

ignition on/off switch

instruments: water temperature
r.p.m.   oil pressure

body made of reinforced fiberglass
for lightness

front spoilers with adjustable angle

air intake to radiator

rear-view mirror

radiator

McLAREN CARS

REYNOLDS
ALUMINUM

fire extinguisher

ventilated disc brakes
(on all wheels)

suspension A-arms

slots cut in tires; when they disappear,
the tire is worn out.

safety belt

rubber fuel tank (one on either side)
carrying total of 44-5 gallons

hub carrier

low-pressure tires

dry-weather treadless tires

The Yardley-McLaren in the paddock ready for the race

The age of the airfoil

Since 1968, automobile race crowds have gradually got used to seeing cars with "wings." These are light metal panels mounted on tubular supports above and behind the driver's head. As you look at them from the side, you see that they are rounded at the edges and tapered like an airplane's wing, but with the main bulge at the bottom instead of at the top.

The cars may also have nose wings mounted at the front, usually just ahead of the wheels. But you may not notice these as quickly because they are smaller, lower and sometimes formed as part of the bodywork. Whatever their shape, style or position, these wings, or airfoils, are not there to give the car a lift but to keep it on the ground.

The performance of a racing car depends very much on its grip on the track — on the friction that develops between the tires and the ground. If there is a great deal of friction, the car is able to take corners fast, to increase its speed under power, and to slow down quickly when the brakes are put on. So each lap is covered in a faster time.

It is possible to improve the tire grip by putting extra weight over the wheels. But this weight would also make it harder for the car to accelerate and slow down. An airfoil will increase the grip simply by creating a downward pressure of air — as shown in the diagrams opposite. And it will do this while adding very little to the actual weight of the car. No wonder designers favor using airfoils, in spite of all their early troubles with them.

Keeping the wheels on the ground

The use of airfoils to help cars hold the road goes back to the 1920's, but they were not introduced into Formula 1 racing until 1968. They became popular at once, but they caused some bad accidents in 1969 because they were not strongly attached. Since then, their size and height have been limited.

Flow of air

March 721G

Matra MS120D

Airfoil is set at angle to airstream, which creates a downward pressure

Flow of air

Airfoil wing

The bulge below forces the airstream to travel farther, and so reduces air pressure. This aids downward thrust by creating a suction effect

End plates to stop the pressure spilling over the sides of the wing

Low pressure area

Total down thrust: 400 lbs.
200 lbs. acting on suspension
200 lbs. acting on suspension

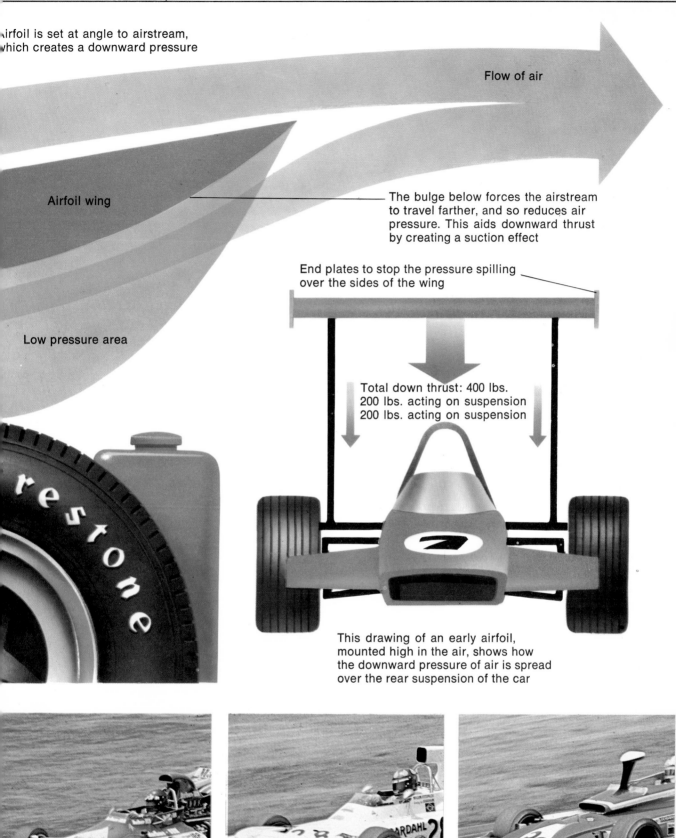

This drawing of an early airfoil, mounted high in the air, shows how the downward pressure of air is spread over the rear suspension of the car

Marlboro-BRM/P160B

Brabham BT 34

Eifelland-March 721

A world of hopeful experiment

The rules of the racing formulas are strict, but they leave the designers with plenty of room for technical experiment. That is why from time to time cars appear with a new shape, a completely different type of engine, or some odd feature which makes everyone stop and stare.

Some of these experiments are taken up by most of the other designers — the airfoil in Formula 1 racing is a good example. Others are failures.

The history of the gas turbine engine shows many of the problems that affect such experiments. This extremely reliable engine (you can see how it works on the opposite page) is widely used to power airplanes and to drive industrial machinery. But the world's first turbocar, the Rover JET 1, was not seen in action until 1950. Two years later it set a world record in its class with a flying kilometer at 151.965 m.p.h. (224.58 k.p.h.).

Since then there have been many attempts to use the gas turbine engine in a race. A Rover-BRM with a 150 b.h.p. gas turbine engine averaged 103 m.p.h. (165.74 k.p.h.) as an unofficial entry in the 1963 Le Mans 24-hour race. The STP-Paxton Turbocar nearly won the 1967 Indianapolis 500, and Lotus has experimented with the engine at Indianapolis and in Formula 1 racing.

Gas turbine engines are easy to run, and give fast acceleration from the starting grid and out of corners, so many designers would like to use them. But their speed is difficult to control.

The fastest vacuum cleaner

Perhaps the strangest car ever to appear on the racing course was the 1970 Chaparral 2J, built by an American designer with many ideas, Jim Hall. It was nicknamed the "vacuum cleaner" because it worked like a hovercraft in reverse, sucking up air from beneath the car instead of blowing it down.

The suction was provided by two fans mounted at the back, and there was a flexible plastic "skirt" around the edge of the car which helped to hold it to the track.

This system held the car so securely to the ground that it could corner at great speed. It set up the fastest lap in the Can-Am race at Watkins Glen, but then was banned from racing.

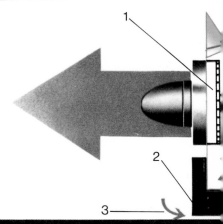

The Stanley Steamers
In the early years of the century, F. E. Stanley built a series of cigar-shaped steam cars nicknamed "Wobblebugs." In 1906 a Wobblebug was driven at 127.66 m.p.h. (205.5 k.p.h.). Next year the same Wobblebug crashed at 150 m.p.h. (240 k.p.h.) and was completely destroyed.
1 High-pressure inlet from boiler
2 Steam expands in cylinder
3 Piston is pushed back, turning wheel
4 Exhaust, which goes into another cylinder to repeat the process
5 At end of each piston stroke a sliding valve reverses the direction of steam flow

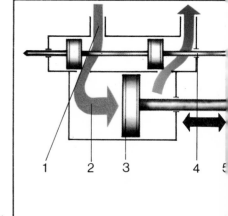

1970 Chaparral 2J
1. Rockwell JL0 two-stroke motor used to drive the fans
2. Lexan "skirt" which reached down to within quarter of an inch of the ground
3. Inflow of air beneath the skirt
4. Path of air sucked out by fans — sufficient to propel the car at 40 m.p.h. (64 k.p.h.) on level ground
5. Downward pressure of over 1000 lbs. (453.59 kilograms) caused by vacuum effect

Lotus 56 gas turbine car
A Lotus 56 was leading into the last 10 laps of the 1968 Indianapolis 500, the second successive year in which a car with a gas turbine engine had almost won the race.

1. Compressor, turned by an electric starter motor, draws in air
2. Air is passed into the combustion chamber
3. Fuel is sprayed in so that it mixes with the compressed air. This ignites to create hot gas
4. Hot gas is passed to the rear turbine, and this provides the motive power which turns the wheels
5. Heat exchanger which uses heat from exhaust to warm up air coming into combustion chamber
6. Exhaust
7. Final drive

There is a "spinning up" period when the electric starter motor continues to run the compressor. But once the gas turbine engine is turning fast enough, it takes over to drive the compressor, and the electric motor is no longer needed.

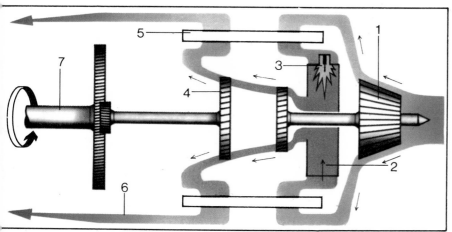

Saving lives at racing courses

Drivers of racing cars know that as speeds increase — especially around corners — so the risk of serious accidents increases. That is why grand prix drivers like Jackie Stewart take safety measures much more seriously nowadays, and have their own association to encourage improvements. Before every grand prix two of its members inspect the course on foot to check all safety precautions.

There are four main areas where lives can be saved — and in most cases *are* saved — by planning ahead. First there is the car itself. It must have a strong roll-over bar to protect the driver in case the car overturns. Gasoline tanks, under the new Formula 1 rules, must be "deformable": that is, be able to bulge without splitting. Automatic fire extinguishers must be fitted.

Next comes the driver's equipment. He needs fireproof overalls and underclothes, a well-designed crash helmet (compulsory since 1948), a face mask which resists flames and fumes, and a complete safety harness to stop him being thrown from the car if he crashes.

Then there is the course. Run-off areas should be provided for the driver to go into if he is in trouble, and gravel to slow down the car. There must be enough guard-rails and netting barriers to protect drivers and spectators.

Finally, if a driver should get seriously injured, he needs the instant help of a mobile hospital.

Cutting down the risks

When a modern racing car travels at up to 200 m.p.h. (321.8 k.p.h.), nothing can be done to make the sport totally safe. All that most racing drivers ask is that unnecessary risks should be removed. One major step forward has been to set up the $125,000 grand prix mobile hospital shown below. It has treated over 300 cases in its first six years, and even major brain surgery has been performed in its operating theatre.

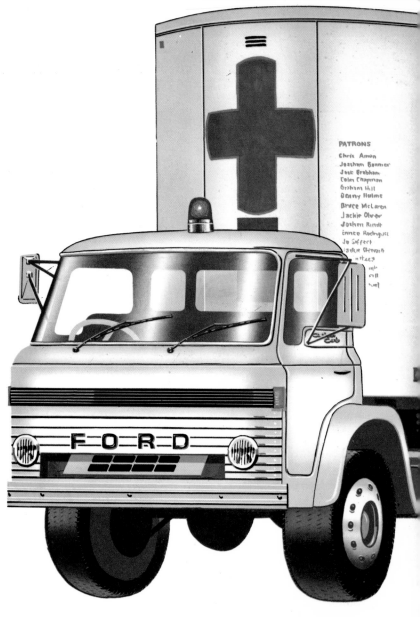

PATRONS
Chris Amon
Joachim Bonnier
Jack Brabham
Colin Chapman
Graham Hill
Denny Hulme
Bruce McLaren
Jackie Oliver
Jochen Rindt
Pedro Rodriguez
Jo Siffert
Jackie Stewart

Although gasoline tanks are now highly protected, there is always the risk of fire after a crash. Fires are fought by extinguishers containing a liquid which turns into a vapor and spreads over the flames, or by a white foam or powder.

Howden Ganley has his blood group (0, Rhesus positive) marked on his overalls.

Heart-reviving machine

Litter bin for dressings

Extractor fans

Ventilating duct

Minor surgery and examination

Refrigerated blood bank cabinet

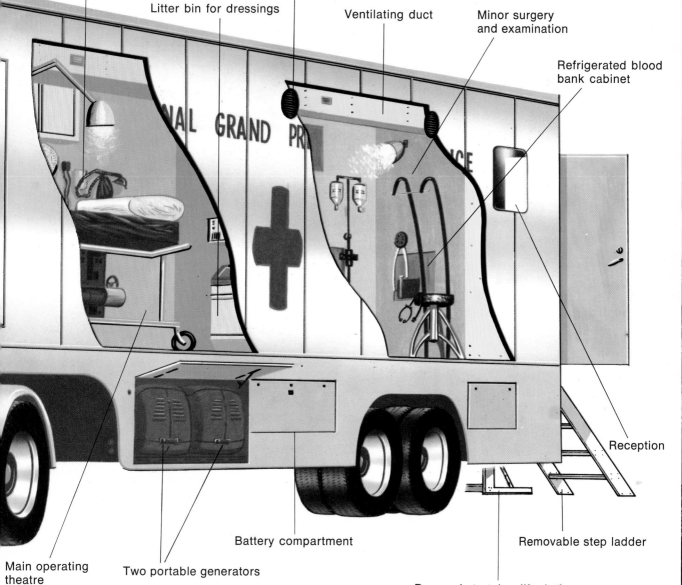

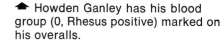

Reception

Main operating theatre

Two portable generators

Battery compartment

Removable step ladder

Powered stretcher lift platform

Great Racing Cars   *4. Into the 1960's*

From the end of the 1950's, a little less was heard of the Italian cars, and new names began to appear on the grand prix scene. Two of the most important were British — the Cooper, and the Lotus of Colin Chapman. They won their races and made new advances which other manufacturers had to follow.

Ford GT40 During the 1960's the Ford Motor Company became a great force in international racing by making a great effort to win one particular race: the Le Mans 24-hour. In the 1964 and 1965 races all three Fords dropped out. But by using a great deal of money and effort, Ford solved the mechanical problems, and in 1966 the Mark 2 Ford GT40's took first, second and third place. They went on to win the race for the next three years.

Lotus 25-Climax Designed by Colin Chapman, the Lotus 25 caused a stir in 1962 by introducing a "monocoque" type of construction to Formula 1 racing. A monocoque body is formed by a single, rounded shell — in this case, of aluminum sheet — instead of being built around the usual chassis frame. Driven by Jim Clark, the 1962 Lotus won three grand prix races. Next year, Clark became world drivers' champion, and Lotus became the constructor's champion.

Cooper T45-Climax In 1959 a small factory in the suburbs of London, run by a father and his son, Charles and John Cooper, became the second British winners of the International Cup for Formula 1 manufacturers. And Jack Brabham, driving a Cooper-Climax, won the world championship for drivers. The unexpected success of this lightweight car with its rear engine made other manufacturers think again.

A career in automobile racing

There is no simple, direct way of becoming a grand prix racing driver. For example, Stirling Moss began by competing in hill-climbs and Jim Clark in club rallies. Jacky Ickx was a trials and John Surtees a road race motor-cyclist, while Jack Brabham and Mario Andretti started in speedway racing, and Emerson Fittipaldi in karting. Graham Hill took the obvious first step of going to an auto racing school.

In almost every case a driver must work his way up to Formula 1 through the lower grades of racing like Formula Ford, Formula Vee and Formulas 2 and 3. But the speed with which he does this varies a great deal from driver to driver. The New Zealander, Chris Amon, began driving Formula 1 at the age of nineteen, but the great Argentinian, Juan Fangio, was 38 before he competed in his first full grand prix season, and was 47 when he retired. Fewer than thirty grand prix drivers can be employed at any time, so that there is almost as much competition to get a drive as there is to win a race.

The one thing all drivers have in common is their determination to race in the highest class they can reach. Graham Hill is a good example of this. He was 24 when he took his first and only racing lesson, but four laps of Brands Hatch in a Formula 3 car gave him all the ambition he needed. He gave up his regular job and then worked for four years at the tracks as a mechanic just to be involved with racing before he got his first drive as a professional.

Rise of a grand prix driver

This is how Paul Carter grew up to be a professional racing driver. Although it is not a true story — there is no Paul Carter in grand prix racing — it gives a true picture of the stages that many drivers pass through.

Paul became an auto racing fan after going with his father to a grand prix.

Paul's father had a friend who competed in sports car races. At 16 Paul was allowed to help him in the pits. His job was to hold out the lap timing board to show the driver his race position.

After passing his driving test at 18, Paul was given a course of racing lessons.

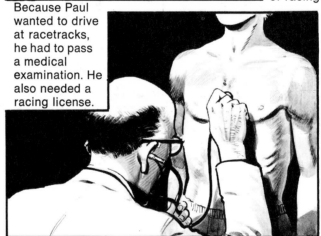
Because Paul wanted to drive at racetracks, he had to pass a medical examination. He also needed a racing license.

Paul next bought fireproof overalls, gauntlet gloves and the best safety helmet he could find. It was worth paying the extra money.

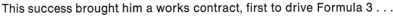
This success brought him a works contract, first to drive Formula 3 . . .

He began collecting racing pictures, learning about the sport from books and helping his father service the family car.

NYK 872

At the racing school.

Then Paul was able to drive twice around the course in the school's Formula Ford car.

Paul did well, but won no races, so after a year his father helped him buy a new $5,000 Formula Ford.

second-
d Formula
cost $1,250.

Two years later he won the national Formula Ford championship.

. . . and after making good progress, Formua 1, at the age of 23.

So came the great day when he won his first grand prix.

Auto racing on a tabletop

You can learn a lot about racing by making model cars. If you build up a collection from model kits, it will help you to identify the different cars more quickly when you visit the course. It will also give you a better idea of how a real car is built.

Making your models from drawings and photographs by cutting out the parts yourself from wood, plastic and metal is more difficult. Some people make a living out of making models like this, which can sell for hundreds of dollars.

Even simple models can be interesting, however, especially if they show how a racing car works. By making the model on the right, you will be able to see for yourself how an airfoil helps a car grip the road.

The kind of tabletop competition known as "slot racing" will also help you to share the skill and excitement of driving in a grand prix. The cars have a tiny electric motor inside them and they move around a course guided by a small peg underneath which fits into a slot in the track.

Each competitor has a hand controller which lets him vary the speed of his car. Just as in a real race, it is not always the fastest car which wins. The "driver" must use his skill in getting around the bends as quickly as he can — but not so fast that his car jumps off the track.

Many people who like slot racing build their own cars and form clubs so that they can race them against other home-made models.

Experiments in design

This working model of a racing car demonstrates the way in which airfoils operate. By adjusting the angle at which they are set you can make the car lift or cling to the ground, travel smoothly or go out of control. You can buy the materials to make it in any hobby shop, and it will only take a couple of hours to put together.

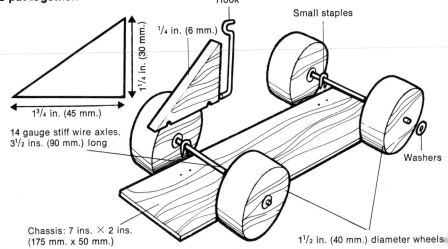

Hook
1/4 in. (6 mm.)
Small staples
1 1/4 in. (30 mm.)
1 3/4 in. (45 mm.)
14 gauge stiff wire axles, 3 1/2 ins. (90 mm.) long
Washers
Chassis: 7 ins. × 2 ins. (175 mm. x 50 mm.)
1 1/2 in. (40 mm.) diameter wheels

Chassis and wheels

Make a chassis by cutting rectangle of 7 ins. x 2 ins. (175 mm. x 50 mm.) from 1.5 mm. ply. Cut two 3 1/2 ins. (90 mm.) lengths of 14 gauge wire for axles, attaching these to chassis with staples, as shown, then sticking them down with epoxy. Add wheels with washer on either side.

Shape triangle from 1/4 in. balsa as in diagram. Cut 2 ins. (50 mm.) length of 20 gauge wire, bending one end into hook and other at right angle. Stick wire to back of triangle with epoxy.

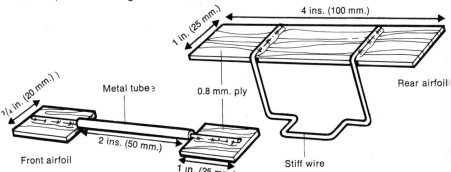

1 in. (25 mm.)
4 ins. (100 mm.)
3/4 in. (20 mm.)
Metal tube
0.8 mm. ply
Rear airfoil
Front airfoil
2 ins. (50 mm.)
1 in. (25 mm.)
Stiff wire

Making the airfoils

From 0.8 mm. ply cut two front airfoils 1 in. × 3/4 in. (25 mm. × 20 mm.) and one rear airfoil 4 ins. × 1 in. (100 mm. × 25 mm.). Slip 4 1/2 ins. (112 mm.) of 20 gauge wire through 2 ins. (50 mm.) tube—pinching tube with pliers if it is too loose. Turn back last 1/4 in. (6 mm.) of wire at each end and fix on front airfoils with epoxy. Glue tube to chassis as shown.

Mount rear airfoil on bent wire frame which is attached to chassis with small square of plywood and screw.

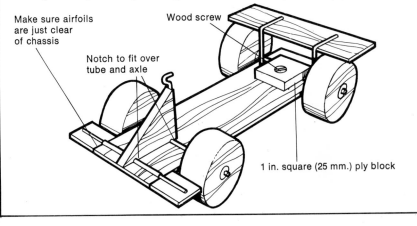

Make sure airfoils are just clear of chassis
Wood screw
Notch to fit over tube and axle
1 in. square (25 mm.) ply block

48

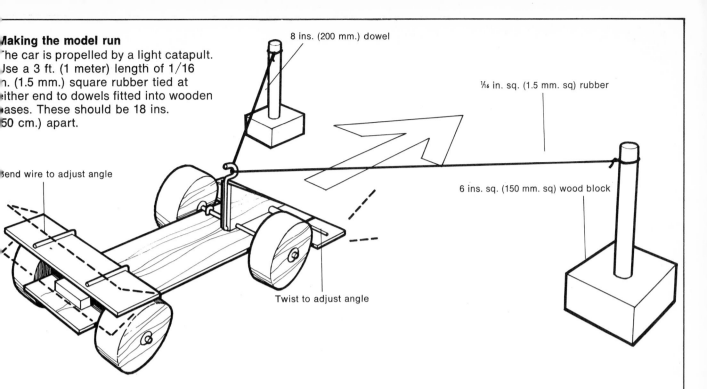

Making the model run

The car is propelled by a light catapult. Use a 3 ft. (1 meter) length of 1/16 in. (1.5 mm.) square rubber tied at either end to dowels fitted into wooden bases. These should be 18 ins. (50 cm.) apart.

8 ins. (200 mm.) dowel

1/16 in. sq. (1.5 mm. sq) rubber

Bend wire to adjust angle

6 ins. sq. (150 mm. sq) wood block

Twist to adjust angle

Try these experiments

Make your test runs on a smooth, level linoleum floor or a large table. If you use a table, put a blanket at the end to stop the car.

First leave the rear airfoil horizontal, but experiment with the angle of the front airfoils. If these are tilted upward, by turning the wire in its tube, the front wheels will begin to lift off the ground. But if they are tilted downward, they will have the opposite effect, and will hold the front of the car down.

Then alter the angle of the rear airfoil by carefully bending the wire uprights with pliers. If it is tilted downward, the rear wheels will be held to the ground. But you will probably find you get the best control by tilting the front airfoils downward as well.

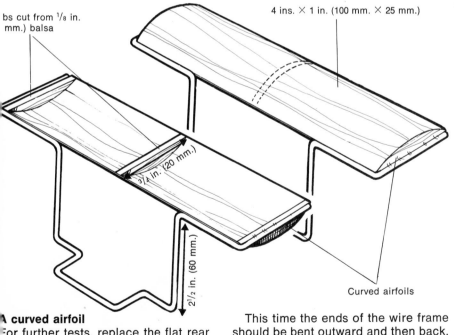

Ribs cut from 1/8 in. (3 mm.) balsa

4 ins. × 1 in. (100 mm. × 25 mm.)

3/4 in. (20 mm.)

2 1/2 in. (60 mm.)

Curved airfoils

A curved airfoil

For further tests, replace the flat rear airfoil with a curved airfoil. Make it from a piece of 1/32 in. (0.8 mm.) balsa sheet cut into a rectangle 4 in. × 1 in. (100 mm. × 25 mm.). To give it a curve, cement it to three ribs of 1/8 in. (3 mm.) balsa wood, as shown. Hold it until the cement has set.

This time the ends of the wire frame should be bent outward and then back, as in diagram. Fasten the airfoil to the frame with epoxy, with the bulge underneath. This will hold down the rear of the car more effectively.

As a final experiment, fix another curved airfoil upside down on wire frame. The rear wheels will lift.

Materials you will need

Plywood in two thicknesses:
  1.5 mm.
  0.8 mm.

Balsa sheet in four thicknesses:
  1/4 in. (6 mm.)
  1/8 in. (3 mm.)
  1/16 in. (1.5 mm.)
  1/32 in. (0.8 mm.)

Steel wire of two thicknesses:
  14 gauge
  20 gauge

Metal tube

Staples

Wood screw

Eight washers

Dowel rod

3 ft. of 1/16 in. (1.5 mm.) square rubber

Five-minute epoxy adhesive

Balsa cement

Four 1 1/4 in. (30 mm.) diameter wheels

Saw

Pliers

Balsa cutting knife

T-square

Pencil

Rallying cry of the enthusiast

Grand prix racing is the sport of the few, but it attracts millions of spectators. Rallying is the pastime of many, but is watched by few.

There are the great motor rallies like the East African Safari, the Monte Carlo—and the World Cup rally described on the right. Here the competitors are often professionals, and the special sections, especially in the mountains, draw big crowds. But for every big event there are hundreds of smaller ones that go unnoticed. Amateur drivers enter them just to test their skill.

A rally must not be confused with a race. The cars do not leave the start together, but at intervals of roughly a minute. They then must travel along a given route, and reach a checkpoint by a certain time.

Drivers lose points by being early as much as by being late at the checkpoint. They may not go faster than an average 30 m.p.h. (42 k.p.h.) on normal roads or 50 m.p.h. (80 k.p.h.) on parkways. The only real speed test comes if they move onto private land. Here they must keep to whatever speed the rally officials have set.

Most rallies are entered by teams comprising a driver and a navigator. But over long distances, when stamina and concentration are vital, both members of the team may have to take turns driving. Even in the smaller amateur rallies, drivers modify their engine, suspension and braking systems before taking part. For the great international rallies the cars are almost rebuilt.

16,000 miles of high adventure

The greatest of all driving endurance tests took place in 1970—the World Cup rally. It began at Wembley stadium, where Britain beat West Germany in the 1966 World Cup football final, and finished, after 16,000 miles of motoring, at the Aztec stadium in Mexico City, where the next World Cup competition was soon to begin.

Ninety-six cars, with drivers from twenty different countries, set off to face almost every kind of driving condition, from the leftover winter snows of Europe to the extreme heat of Ecuador.

↑ The start at Wembley, London, where the 1966 World Cup football final had been played.

April in London
The field that set out from Wembley on Sunday, April 19, was extremely mixed. There were teams backed by automobile manufacturers, teams from the army, from newspapers and television, as well as partnerships of private drivers. Among the more unusual starters were a beach buggy, a minicar and two Rolls-Royces.

The manufacturers' cars may have been the best prepared, but even the private entries had been expensively modified. By the time workshop bills had been paid, spares and material had been bought, and the cars had been out to survey in advance the European sections of the course, every serious entry was faced with a cost of $25,000 or more. This was high adventure, but at a high price.

↑ Sofia, capital of Bulgaria and the most easterly checkpoint on the long journey.

Through Europe
You can follow the course of the rally on the map below. After the first checkpoint at Dover, the cars crossed the English Channel by ferry to Boulogne, and eastward across France and Germany.

In East Europe, nearing the Bulgarian capital, Sofia, they ran into heavy spring rain. Turning south into Yugoslavia, they found so much snow that some sections had to be cancelled. And then in Spain they came across the early summer dust. Within a week they had passed through the weather conditions of three seasons.

Mexico City, Finish: May 26, 1970

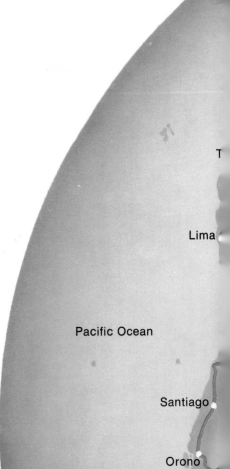

T

Lima

Pacific Ocean

Santiago

Orono

At Lisbon docks

Of the ninety-six cars to start from Wembley, only seventy-two reached Lisbon within the time limit on the following Sunday. They were put aboard the *Derwent* for a leisurely twelve-day voyage across the Atlantic, while their drivers, co-drivers and navigators rested before flying to Rio de Janeiro.

Zasada and Wachkowski of Poland raise dust from their speeding Escort.

⬆ The two Finns, Makinen and Staepelaeve, take a rocky precipice in their newspaper-sponsored Escort.

To the Inca trails

On May 8 it was winter in Rio de Janeiro (since that city lies south of the Equator), but the temperature was a pleasant 90°F (32°C) when the rally began its second section.

During the first day's stage ten cars dropped out on the rough country roads of Brazil. But worse was to come: 200 miles of dirt roads across the Pampas; the crossing of the Andes into Peru; the 14,000-foot (4,437 meters) La Paz climb.

⬆ The winning cars, led by Hannu Mikkola (Finland) and Gunnar Palm (Sweden) in their Ford Escort, make their victory parade through Mexico City.

Mexican finish

After the marathon journey—which tested the strength of the cars and the stamina of the drivers almost to breaking point—twenty-three cars, less than a quarter of those that set out, reached Mexico City. The winners were the Scandinavians, Mikkola of Finland and Palm of Sweden, who had driven a Ford Escort. It had been a triumph for their skill, courage and stubbornness.

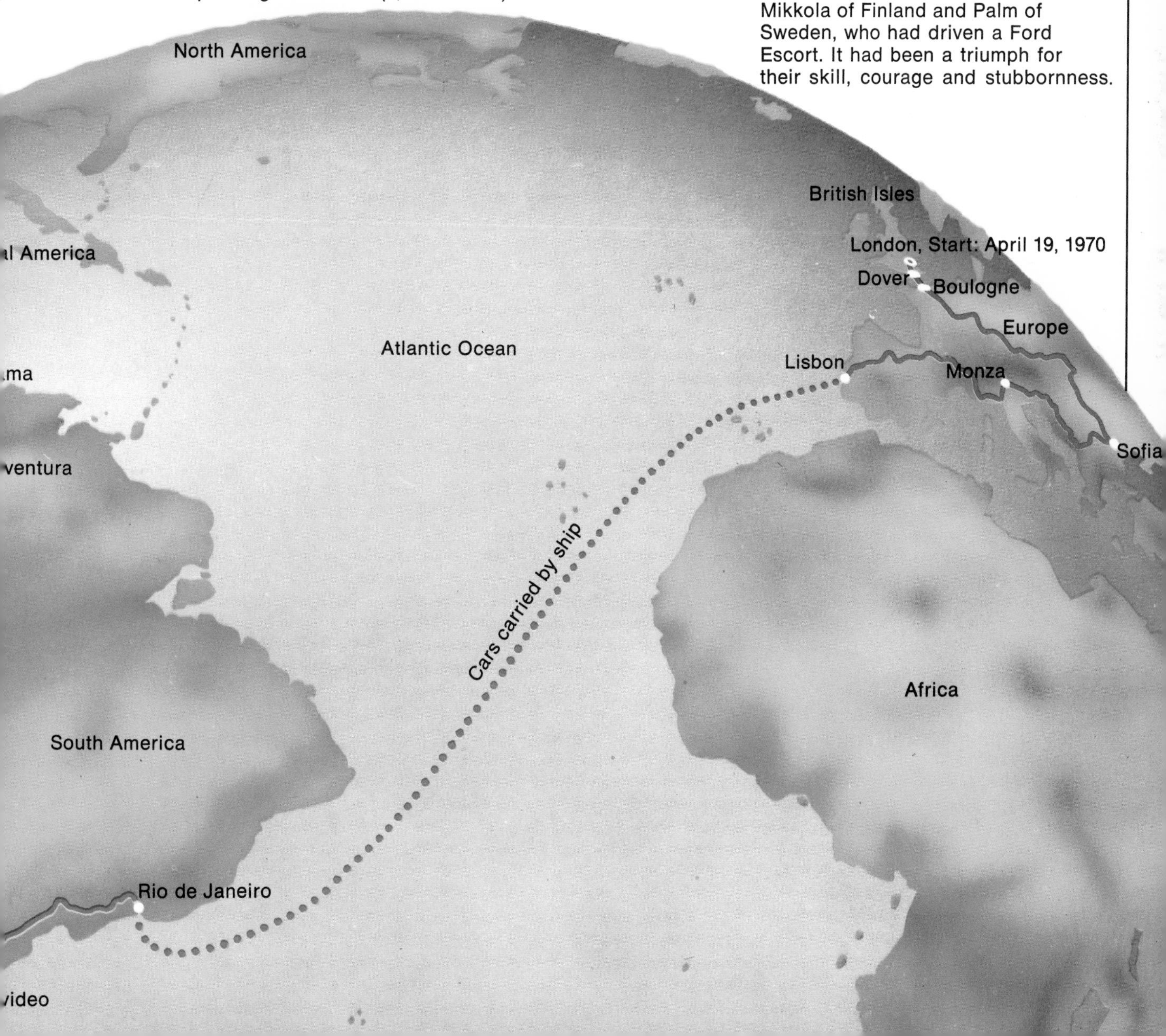

North America

British Isles

London, Start: April 19, 1970

Dover Boulogne

Europe

al America

Atlantic Ocean

Lisbon   Monza

ma

Sofia

ventura

Cars carried by ship

Africa

South America

Rio de Janeiro

video

Dragsters – all speed and smoke

The strange machines pictured on this page are dragsters. They travel in a straight line, smoke pouring from behind them, for only a quarter of a mile (405 m.). But within that short distance, from a standing start, they can get up to 200 m.p.h. (322 k.p.h.), and the fastest of them has done that quarter of a mile in only 5.91 secs.

Drag racing began in the United States in the early 1950's. It grew out of a craze for souping up old cars and challenging others to a street race. To "drag" someone meant that you issued a challenge to him.

By 1955 the sport had left the back streets because special tracks, or "strips," had been built. There are now about 500 of these in the United States and they are used by more than half a million drivers. The sport has spread to Europe.

Each race is held between two cars, the winner going on to compete in the next round.

As the dragsters approach the starting line, with their engines crackling loudly and flames leaping from their exhaust pipes, they have a "burn-out" on resin or household bleach sprinkled on the track to clean the tires.

There are starting lights on what is known as the "Christmas tree." These change from yellow to amber to green, and in a cloud of smoke produced by the burning rubber of the tires, the cars start their short, spectacular journey. They reach top speed just before the finish, and the driver must send out a parachute to bring the car to a stop.

Strange fuels and funny cars

There are several different sorts of dragsters: the "funny cars" which have plastic bodies; the gas and fuel dragsters which are 13 ft. (4 m.) long and have a rail chassis with no body. Their front wheels are smaller than those at the rear, and only 3 in. (8 cm.) wide; the Double A fuel dragsters which run on a fuel mixture of alcohol and 90 per cent nitromethane; and jet cars which have recorded 270 m.p.h. (432 k.p.h.) but are used mainly for exhibitions.

Funny car

Street altered

Fuel dragster

A quarter-mile in six seconds

"Burn-out" with resin-soaked tires to clean and warm them.

Starting grid with photo-electric eye

Tires spun to achieve maximum grip (the cars have only one forward gear)

Peak velocity achieved—about 200 m.p.h. (322 k.p.h.)

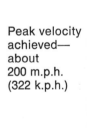

Electronic relay system for timing

Driver "pops the chute" to slow car down

△ Flame-out. Just as well the driver has fireproof clothing

Putting horsepower behind the kart

Like dragster racing, karting began in the United States. It was brought to England in 1959 and has gradually spread all over Europe.

A kart is usually just a frame without any bodywork, and may not be more than 72 ins. (1.829 m.) in length. It has no suspension, and the driver is seated only an inch or so (2-3 cms.) from the ground. The simplest version is driven by a lawnmower engine and has no gears. More advanced models have 200 c.c. or 250 c.c. motorcycle engines.

The earliest kart races were sprints, with few events of over twelve miles (19.3 kms). Now there are races lasting nine hours in which an average speed of over 74 m.p.h. (119.09 k.p.h.) is maintained. Some karts are capable of 100 m.p.h. (160.94 k.p.h.) laps.

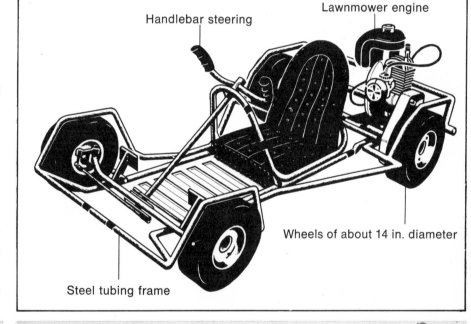

Handlebar steering

Lawnmower engine

Wheels of about 14 in. diameter

Steel tubing frame

Cornering on the flat

Start of a race

Competing off the beaten track

Grand prix driving is only for professionals, and even for sports car racing at an international level you either need lots of money of your own or the backing of a sponsor in the automobile industry.

That is why there is such a growing interest in the kind of events illustrated on this page that take place far from the racing courses and cater to amateurs who have no money to waste. There are 22,000 people in Britain alone who take out competition licenses issued by the Royal Automobile Club, the national body which is in charge of auto sport. Some of them may intend to compete in track races, but the great majority want to take part in such things as autocross, hillclimbs and trials.

At this amateur level, driving probably costs no more than taking up, say, photography seriously. A car which is suitable for trials can be bought for as little as $1,000. And at most autocross, hill climb and sprint events — as well as at trials — there are opportunities for the driver to compete in his family car if he wishes.

He may need to adapt the car to compete more successfully, of course, changing to heavier tires, souping up the engine and fitting roll-over bars and a full seat harness. The rules may force him to make other slight changes to the car. But most competitors enjoy working on their cars. This is a far cry from grand prix racing with its teams of mechanics. It is the world of do-it-yourself.

Up the hill, and over the grass

These auto sports may be very different, but they have one thing in common. Their object is to make life more difficult for the driver, and for his car. Climbing a long, twisting hill, turning sharply on wet grass, driving through obstacles with scarcely any clearance on either sides—these are the tests they set the competitor.

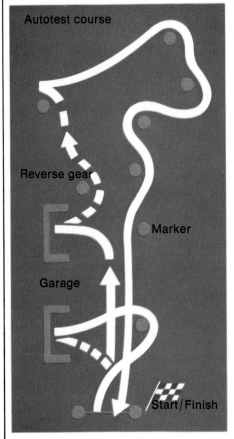

Autotest course
Reverse gear
Garage
Marker
Start/Finish

Sprints, slaloms and autotests
Sprints and slaloms usually take place on an empty airfield, and in both events the drivers start at intervals. The driver in a sprint must do a faster time than the others over so many laps of a course where a tiny error of line or a badly timed gear change can cost him victory. In a slalom he must weave his way through.

Autotests need less space, for the course is less than 200 yds. (182.88 m.) in length, although much more complicated. Drivers must go through narrow openings, take sharp turns, and in some places drive in reverse through obstacles.

Trials
Trials are a test of getting up rough, muddy hills—often with stones, streams and tree trunks in the way— without coming to a stop. In most trials there are ten or twelve of these uphill sections to be tackled in turn. Speed does not matter, but points are lost for leaving the course or stopping.

Both special trials machines and family cars can take part. The driver carries a passenger, or "bouncer," who has the job of bouncing on his seat, or putting his weight over the rear wheel to stop it spinning in the soft earth.

Autocross and Rallycross

Autocross, which began in the late 1940's, is a short speed event held in a field instead of on a racing track. It is exciting because the slippery grass and mud make it more difficult for the driver to control the car. The course is usually a course of half a mile (804.5 m.) which the drivers cover three or four times. Usually two cars start at a time, and the fastest in each round, whether or not they win their heat, go on to the next round.

Rallycross, which was invented as a television entertainment in 1966, is very similar. But here the course consists of road as well as rough country, like the special section in a motor rally, and four cars start at once. All types of cars take part, but the most popular in both sports are minis.

Adapted for rallycross

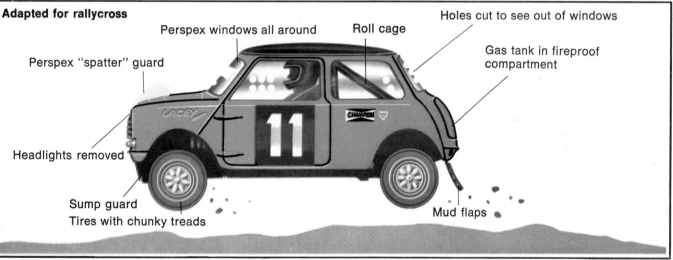

Perspex windows all around

Roll cage

Holes cut to see out of windows

Perspex "spatter" guard

Gas tank in fireproof compartment

Headlights removed

Sump guard

Tires with chunky treads

Mud flaps

↟ Hillclimbing

One of the oldest types of auto sport was hillclimbing which became popular in Britain because ordinary road racing was banned from the public roads. Instead, drivers took their cars to a narrow, winding upward hill—either on private property or in a lonely place—and set off at intervals to see who could get to the top in the shortest time.

British hillclimbs are usually only 1000 yards (914.39 meters) in length, and often shorter. But the European Hillclimb Championship for sports cars is on courses of from three miles (4.83 kms) to twelve miles (19.31 kms).

Great Racing Cars *5. Up to the present day*

As racing gains momentum in the 1970's, costs rise. The engine of the
Porsche 917, shown below, alone costs $60,000. During the next ten years
automobile racing must face the problem of curbing the expense of the sport
so that it will still be possible for new manufacturers to participate.

Ferrari 312 B-3
Newest shape on the grand prix
courses: the Ferrari introduced to meet
the new Formula 1 for 1973. It is
another car for which the monocoque
body design was chosen, and carried
out in England. Notice Ferrari's
famous symbol, the prancing horse,
just below the cockpit.

Porsche 917-10K CanAm
This 5-liter turbo-charged version of
the Porsche 917 won six out of the nine
races which made up the 1972 CanAm
(short for Canadian-American) series.

The 12-cylinder Porsche 917 is the
most powerful sports car ever built.
Introduced in 1969, it has won nearly
all the great endurance tests, including
the Le Mans and Daytona 24-hours.

Eagle-Offenhauser
Driven by Bobby Unser, the Offenhauser-powered Eagle was the unexpected winner of the 1968 Indianapolis 500. Most people believed that cars with the new turbine engines would win the race, but one after another they dropped out. Unser took first place and set a record average of 152.88 m.p.h. (246.07 k.p.h.).

The future of automobile racing

Automobile racing is always changing. Officials see to that by altering the main formulas every six years or so, and by changing the rules slightly almost every season. This gives designers and drivers new problems to solve, and keeps the sport alive.

The designers, too, bring in changes of their own. They introduced the rear engine, the monocoque body, and airfoils into Formula 1 racing — not to meet the organizers' rules but because they thought these new features would bring their cars better results. The rules still leave plenty of room for experiment, and over the next ten years designers will certainly be trying out new materials, new types of engine, new aerodynamic theories.

The rising cost of automobile racing, especially in Formula 1, may also bring about changes in the sport. Each season it becomes more expensive to produce a successful grand prix car, and to pay the high fees which leading drivers demand. This makes life hard for the manufacturers who run teams.

At the same time, drivers are asking for better safety measures. This has two results. The course owners must spend more money on improvements — putting up safety fences and removing obstacles at the side of the track — which leaves them less money to pay the teams. At the same time, as more barriers are put up, spectators are pushed back and see less of the racing. We may yet see formulas designed to produce slower, cheaper and safer cars.

A car for the 1980's?

What will tomorrow's Formula 1 racing car look like? Nobody can say for certain, but the car illustrated below includes ideas that designers are working on at the moment.

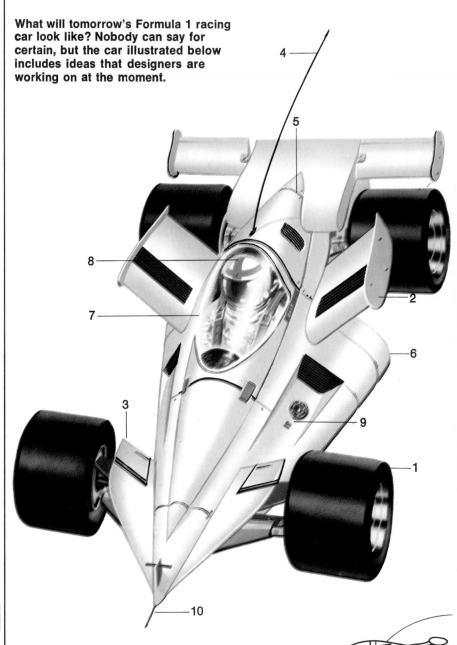

1 Four-wheel drive. There may also be a move toward wider tires
2 Oil radiators mounted as wings
3 Wings which change their angle to the airstream. The angle is controlled by (10)
4 Aerial to keep driver in radio contact with his team at the pits
5 Wankel rotary engine with automatic gears. This engine is smaller and so allows designers to produce lighter, more compact cars
6 Wedge-shaped body to aid airflow
7 "Bubble" canopy to enclose driver

8 Safety helmet which covers the head completely. Provides oxygen supply so that driver is not overcome by fumes if a fire breaks out
9 Pressure refuelling tanks which can be filled more quickly at the pits
10 Airflow indicator which will automatically change the angle of the wings (3)

Glossary of automobile racing terms

A-arm American term for wishbone (see below).

Anti-roll bar A device fitted to the suspension to cut down on the amount that a car rolls at the corners.

Aquaplaning Losing grip on the track and sliding over the wet surface after heavy rain.

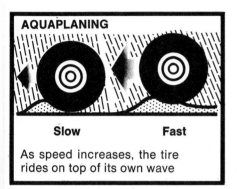

AQUAPLANING

Slow   Fast

As speed increases, the tire rides on top of its own wave

Armco guard rail A type of corrugated steel barrier which is put up so that a car cannot run off the track after an accident.

Back-marker One of the last cars in the race and in danger of being lapped by the leaders.

B.h.p. (brake horse power) The power of an engine, which is measured on a machine called a dynamometer.

Blow-up Engine failure.

Brew up To catch fire.

Bulkhead A partition in the body of the car. In cars of monocoque design bulkheads play an important part in strengthening the body and holding it rigid. The bulkheads to the front and rear of the driver may also be fire-proofed to prevent flames from the engine reaching the gasoline tanks in case of an accident.

Catch tank A tank which catches any overflow of water or oil and so prevents it dropping on to the track.

Chicane An S-bend put into a straight section of the track. It may be used to force drivers to reduce speed as a safety measure, or to give an extra advantage to skillful drivers.

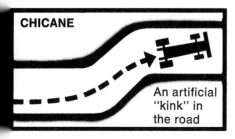

CHICANE

An artificial "kink" in the road

Come-in signal An arrow held up by a member of the pit crew to ask a driver to come into the pits on the next lap.

Dice Hard, close struggle for position between two or more cars.

Dummy grid Area just before the starting grid (see below) where cars get in their correct positions and start their engines.

Formula libre Type of race in which cars of any formula may compete.

Full bore Flat out.

Gas turbine engine Form of engine used a great deal in airplanes and in industry which came into use in motor sports during the 1960's.

Go into the country Leave the track, either by accident or to avoid an accident.

Grand Epreuve A world championship qualifying round for Formula 1. Also used to describe some other major international races.

Jump-start Attempt to gain advantage over the other drivers by moving across the starting line before the judge's flag is down. The driver who makes a jump-start is usually given a penalty of one minute.

Hairy Wild and sometimes dangerous driving.

Lap Length of the course, beginning and ending at the starting line. To lap another driver means to gain a lap upon him and pass him.

Lap of honor Last lap made by the winning driver before he pulls into the pits. It is made so that the crowd can see him once more and applaud him.

Lose it Lose control of the car.

Muffler Device for silencing noise.

Overalls Clothing worn by the driver, usually treated with chemicals to make them fire resistant.

Over-rev To drive an engine at more than the number of revolutions for which it was built; this can make the engine break down.

Pace notes Notes for the use of a rally driver, telling him the length and the spacing of bends on the course, and the speed at which he should drive through them.

Paddock Area near the track where cars are prepared for racing.

Pit-stop Visit to the pits for fuel or servicing during a race.

Pole position The best place at the front of the starting grid. It is normally given to the driver who gained the fastest lap in practice.

Rolling start Starting method used in Can Am and Indianapolis racing, in which the cars approach the starting line in formation behind an official car, and are then waved on to begin the race.

Run out of road Fail to take corner and leave the track.

Shunt Accident, crash.

Silencer Term for muffler used in the UK.

South Pole The worst position on the starting grid.

Special stage In a rally, a section of private track, or a road closed to other traffic, in which cars are timed to the second.

Spin, spin off Lose control of the car, which spins around on the track or leaves the course.

Starting grid The area on which the cars are held for a few seconds in their correct starting order after leaving the dummy grid (see above). They then move off after being given the starter's signal.

Supercharged With the fuel-air mixture forced into the engine to produce more power.

Ton 100 m.p.h.

Warming-up lap Lap driven by the cars before the start of the race.

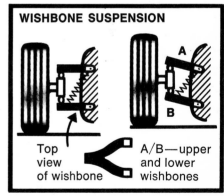

WISHBONE SUSPENSION

Top view of wishbone

A/B—upper and lower wishbones

Wishbone A part of the suspension system, shaped like a chicken's wishbone, which keeps the wheels upright. More commonly known as the A-arm.

Yump Scandinavian term used in rally driving to describe a bump big enough to throw the car into the air.

Index

Numbers in heavy type refer to
illustrations
Entries in italics refer to cars

Illustration credits

Artists
Hargrave Hands
John Hutchinson
David Jeffries
Bill Lacey
Michael Roffe

Photographs and prints
Alsport International
Hugh Bishop
Competition Car
Daily Telegraph
Mary Evans Picture Library
Fox Photos
Foulis and Co.
Roland Groom
Peter Mackertich
Michael Marchant Ltd.
Lord Montague of Beaulieu Library
Motosport
Roger Phipps
Paul Popper
J. Spencer Smith
Syndication International

Projects
Ron Warring

PARAGUAY Gs.18,15
BUGATTI 368 1979 AEREO

2 DH. POSTAGE
CLAY REGAZZONI CHI
AJMAN

PARAGUAY Gs.0.75
PORSCHE CORREO

10 DH. BLITZEN BENZ
1911
AJMAN POSTAGE

PARAGUAY Gs.50,00
MERCEDES 1924 AEREO

1962
XI e GRAND PRIX AUTOMOBILE
MONACO 1.00

MONACO
0,05 1967
MERCEDES - 1936

60 AVUS 1921-1971
DEUTSCHE BUNDESPOST BERLIN

TANZANIA UGANDA KENYA Sh1'30

II JUGOSLOVENSKI ALPSKI RALLYE 1953
70
FNR JUGOSLAVIJA

MONACO
0,01 1967
BUGATTI 1931

XXXIV e RALLYE MONTE CARLO
MINSK
MONTE CARLO
MONACO 1965 1.00

PARAGUAY Gs.0.20
CARP
BRABHAM CORREO

1 RL AIR MAIL
GRAHAM HILL GB
AJMAN

PARAGUAY Gs.0.50
MATRA-SIMCA-MS 660 CORREO

PARAGUAY   Gs.0.10

FERRARI   CORREO

10 DH.   POSTAGE

JACKIE STEWART (GB)

AJMAN

PARAGUAY   Gs.0.30

HONDA   CORREO

STOCKHOLM   1.00

XXX B   RALLYE MONTE-CARLO 1961

15 DH.   OPEL RACINGCAR   1913/14

AJMAN   POSTAGE

EAST AFRICAN SAFARI RALLY

TANZANIA UGANDA KENYA   50

MONACO   0,02   1967

ALFA ROMEO - 1932

PARAGUAY   Gs.12.45

MASERATI - 8 CTF 1938   AEREO

REPUBLIQUE ISLAMIQUE DE MAURITANIE
POSTE AERIENNE 1969 * COURSE AUTOMOBILE LONDRES-SYDNEY

AUSTRALIE   70 F

LESOTHO

12½c   ROOF OF AFRICA RALLY   12½c

MANAMA
DEPENDENCY OF AJMAN

ALFA ROMEO P 2

15 DH.   POSTAGE

PARAGUAY   Gs.0.15

BRM   CORREO

1 DH.   POSTAGE

JACQUES ICKX (B)

AJMAN

PARAGUAY   Gs.0.25

MARCH   CORREO